chocolate holidays

ALSO BY ALICE MEDRICH

BitterSweet: Recipes and Tales from a Life in Chocolate (Artisan)

Alice Medrich's Cookies and Brownies

Chocolate and the Art of Low-Fat Desserts

Cocolat: Extraordinary Desserts

chocolate holidays | alice medrich

unforgettable desserts for every season

photography
michael lamotte

ARTISAN
New York

Photographs copyright © 2001 by Michael Lamotte
Styling by Sara Slavin
Ice Cream Styling by M. Susan Broussard

This book first appeared in hardcover as *A Year in Chocolate:
Four Seasons of Unforgettable Desserts* (Warner Books, a Time
Warner Company, 2001).

Published by Artisan
A Division of Workman Publishing, Inc.
708 Broadway
New York, New York 10003-9555
www.artisanbooks.com

Library of Congress Cataloging-in-Publication Data
Medrich, Alice
    Chocolate holidays : unforgettable desserts for every
    season / Alice Medrich ; photography, Michael Lamotte
      p. cm.
    Includes index.
    ISBN-13: 978-1-57965-290-6
    ISBN-10: 1-57965-290-5
      1. Cookery (Chocolate) 2. Chocolate desserts.
      3. Holiday cookery. I. Title.

    TX767.C5M4298 2005
    641.6'374--dc22

First Artisan paperback edition, 2005
10 9 8 7 6 5 4 3 2 1
Printed in China

to lucy

ACKNOWLEDGMENTS

Writing a cookbook is a challenge and a joy, every single time. Many of my accomplices are previous offenders! Warm thanks once again to my assistant, Maya Klein, for her creative mind, hard work, and friendship. And to Warner Books, thanks for making it happen for the fourth time. As always, I am grateful beyond words to Susan Derescky for her copy editing. Thanks again to photographer Michael Lamotte at Michael Lamotte Studio for fabulous photos and to stylist Sara Slavin for the clarity of her vision. Thanks, finally, to a great agent, Jane Dystel.

x   recipe list

xii   introduction

xiv   details make a difference

1   fall

27   winter

61   spring

85   summer

108   dressing up desserts

112   tempering chocolate

114   ingredients

116   chocolate and cocoa for baking
       and dessert making

120   equipment

124   resources

125   index

recipe list

fall

Chocolate Peanut Butter Layer Cake

Chocolate Sour Cream Layer Cake

Mocha Marjolaine

Honey-Drizzled Chocolate Cheese Fritters

Honey Walnut Tart

Chocolate Cranberry Bread Pudding

Ripe Figs with Mint Ganache

Gingerbread with Milk Chocolate Chunks

Chocolate Pecan Pie

Maya's Day of the Dead Cookies

Chocolate-Dipped Caramel Apples

winter

Chocolate Banana Blintzes

Winter Solstice Cookies

Chocolate Latkes

Chocolate Cream Puffs with Spun Sugar

Chocolate Hazelnut Roulade

Bittersweet Chocolate Truffles

Very Rich Hot Chocolate

Chocolate Cranberry Babka

Black-and-White Apricot Pecan Cake

Chocolate Blini with Berry Caviar

Chocolate-Laced Holiday Stollen

Breakfast Valentines

Hot Chocolate Soufflés

Irish Coffee Chocolate Mousse

The Ultimate Flourless Chocolate Cake

Chocolate Mardi Gras Fondue

spring

Chocolate Hamantaschen

Passover Brownies

Passover Chocolate Nut Sponge Torte

Passover Gâteau au Chocolat

Mocha Marble Cheesecake

Chocolate Easter Baskets

Coffee Meringue Mushrooms

Ice Cream Easter Eggs

Giant Krispy Egg

Chocolate-Dipped Strawberries

White Chocolate–Lemon Cheesecake

Apricot Orange Wedding Cakes

White Chocolate Glaze

Chocolate Banana Waffles for Dad

summer

Independence Day Sundaes

Chocolate Sauce

Boardwalk Bananas

Mini Blackberry Caramel Cheesecakes

Strawberry Mocha Meringue

The New Strawberries and Cream

Chocolate Pound Cake

White Chocolate–Banana Nectarine Trifle

White Chocolate Custard Sauce

Hot Waffle Ice Cream Sandwiches

Hazelnut Chocolate Meringue with Blackberries

Fastest Fudge Cake

Fast Fudge Frosting

introduction

I began this book with the idea of creating a collection of simple, elegant desserts—all made with chocolate—for each holiday on the calendar. But I quickly found excuses for more desserts. What about birthdays, graduations, picnics, luncheons, tea, and dinner parties? Official holidays punctuate the year like a festive centerpiece, but no one should wait for a date to indulge in chocolate. Eating chocolate is, after all, a celebration all its own. So I have included recipes that honor the influence of the seasons—for any occasion—as well as hallowed holiday favorites.

Chocolate is a year-round passion for me, and I eat it every single day. But my taste for this exalted food is not the same in winter as in spring; My appetite is tempered by the mood and color of the seasons. Fortunately, chocolate is infinitely adaptive: dramatic, seductive, and playful.

Excess may be the stuff of chocolate fantasies, but restraint is sometimes the secret ingredient. It takes only a slick of chocolate glaze to add glory to an autumn tart rich with honey and walnuts; just a lacing of chopped chocolate to dress up a fruit-filled Christmas stollen. A little burst of chocolate sauce in a hot crepe with bananas is more seductive than a chocolate blintz with chocolate filling. Too much chocolate simply destroys the essence of pecan pie. And there is no chocolate variation that could dethrone my mother's Thanksgiving apple pie.

Even in California, where seasons are subtle, I long for robust flavors at the very first scent of fall. With the approach of Rosh Hashanah, Halloween, and Thanksgiving I want juicy pears, plump figs, hot ginger, and warm spices. I crave slow-cooked main dishes, toasted nuts, tart apples, and almost anything caramelized for dessert. The nutty sweetness of a Honey Walnut Tart is accented perfectly with chocolate glaze, and the welcome surprise of Chocolate-Dipped Caramel Apples puts a new (and sumptuous) twist on a Halloween favorite.

Winter is a grand excuse to abandon restraint in favor of the richest, deepest, and darkest chocolate of all, warming and sensual. The chill in the air invites excess—recipes that celebrate chocolate purely for chocolate's sake add to the glow of Christmas and the allure of Valentine's Day. In the dead of winter, nothing is more sublime than the intense and relentless wave of bittersweet, found in my best Bittersweet Chocolate Truffles, Ultimate Flourless Chocolate Cake, and Hot Chocolate Soufflés. Here, deep, dark chocolate reigns supreme with minimal sugar and no distraction, save for the odd dollop of cream or necklace of raspberries to make it even more intense by contrast.

Spring demands change, a lightening influence, a playful demeanor, a little humor. Easter baskets, ice cream Easter eggs, and trompe l'oeil mushrooms fill that bill. And why not brownies for Passover? In spring, even a die-hard lover of bittersweet might stray to explore the nuances of white chocolate. I lavish extra attention on white chocolate here, because it is ordinarily my least favorite. If you share my prejudice, set it aside and taste white chocolate again. It is subtle in spring with a touch of lemon in my White Chocolate–Lemon Cheesecake. It is divine in summer, infused with fresh mint and spooned over ripe strawberries, paired with coffee meringues in Strawberry Mocha Meringues, or in stunning Mini Blackberry Caramel Cheesecakes.

Summer holidays are few, but on and after the Fourth of July, we picnic, barbecue, mark birthdays, and get married outdoors. In sultry weather, chocolate does not leap first to mind, but it's perfect to tantalize lethargic taste buds with seductive contrast: hot and cold, crisp and creamy, tart and rich. I always enjoy the subtleties of chocolate and summer berries and fruits. And not-so-subtle Boardwalk Bananas prove that chocolate can be a temptress even when the atmosphere is steamy.

When I owned a bakery many years ago, I could produce a masterpiece in no time by simply strolling through the kitchen collecting components. Now I am more conscious of the home cook's time, space, and ingredients; I keep it simple. I won't compromise on flavor, texture, or ingredients: Excellent chocolate, fresh dairy products, sipping-quality liquors, fresh fruits, and nuts are still my essential ingredients. But I want fewer steps—and variety. A bûche de noël that takes less than an hour belongs in any dessert maker's arsenal, and simple-but-superb chocolate truffles are my salvation all year—as holiday gifts or after-dinner sweets. I also like recipes that young cooks can enjoy: a rustic-looking Easter basket made of chocolate-coated pretzels or a giant "prehistoric"-looking dinosaur Easter egg for kids of every age. Meanwhile, I treasure a fast-as-lightning fudge layer cake recipe for spur-of-the-moment celebrations, and a great chocolate sauce to drizzle over ice cream or recruit for fondue. Do-ahead chocolate soufflés take only minutes to make and are elegant as can be. Meringues, which keep for weeks, are an instant summer dessert kit.

When I cook at home for any occasion, dessert must look divine, but not necessarily as though it stepped out of a fancy patisserie. Occasionally, I pull out the stops with a little spun sugar or gold leaf—lots of fun and simpler than you think—but most of the desserts in this collection speak for themselves, with an elegant simplicity. Among them, you will find recipes to make again and again, on holidays and every day. I wish you the great pleasure of serving desserts that elicit sighs and moans, or even reverent silence, no matter what the season. Bon appétit.

details make a difference

I have watched enough good cooks in their own kitchens to know that dessert making, working with chocolate, and baking in particular are different from general cooking. Small, simple, but nonintuitive details can significantly alter results. Unlike the cook, the baker cannot usually taste and adjust or taste and repair as he or she bakes a cake. Knowing which details make the difference can set you free to be as creative and playful as you like, without sorry surprises.

READY SET GO: MISE EN PLACE

Mise en place is a lovely sounding French phrase meaning "put into place" or "set up." Have you seen TV chefs with all their ingredients measured out in little dishes before the cooking begins? That's mise en place! You might think, "If I had someone to set out all my ingredients, cooking would be easy." And you would be right.

I am a recent convert to and a true believer in the ritual of mise en place. The act of setting out and measuring ingredients aids focus. It promotes attention, thus elevating your connection to the task. It clears your mind of distractions. You will know, before you even start a recipe, that you have all of the ingredients and equipment that you need, and you will be less likely to measure incorrectly or forget to include an ingredient in the batter. This is a boon to anyone who has family members, pets, or friends in the house, is over the age of forty-five, or who is in any other way human.

Many desserts turn out best when recipe steps are performed in sequence, without interruption. Mise en place ensures that once you begin the recipe you will not have to run to the store, search the sandbox for the sifter, or rummage in the pantry for a particular pan while your beautiful batter deflates. Baking and dessert making will become calmer and more pleasurable. Many find it meditative. Your desserts will be more spectacular. You will want to make them again and again and again.

Tenderness in baking is usually the result of simple, but superb technique—proper measuring, mixing, and timing. It's easier than you think.

Toughness results from badly measured flour, the wrong flour (bread flour or whole grain flour rather than all-purpose or cake flour), and too much mixing after the flour has been added to the moist ingredients in the batter. Baking at too high a temperature or too low a temperature or for too long can also cause tough cakes, cookies, pancakes, waffles. The fix? Read and follow the recipe carefully. Use the type of flour called for in the recipe, measure it accurately, mix only as directed, and check your oven and timer.

MEASUREMENT MATTERS

Inaccurate measurements do not always spoil desserts. You may use a liberal hand with raisins, nuts, chocolate chips, coconut, or even vanilla. Feel free to substitute dried fruits and nuts for one another and to experiment with extracts and flavors. That's the creative part of baking.

But for tender cakes with a perfect crumb, please measure the baking soda, baking powder, salt, and, most of all, flour carefully. Baking is not as forgiving as general cooking, even—and especially—when it comes to simple recipes. If cakes are tough, dry, doughy, or leaden, chances are your flour measurement was inaccurate.

A cup of all-purpose flour can weigh anywhere from 4 to 6 ounces depending on whether or not it was sifted before measuring or whether it was packed firmly into the cup. That 2-ounce (50 percent) discrepancy can make the difference between a moist, light poem of a cake and a doorstop.

HOW TO MEASURE FLOUR FOR THE RECIPES IN THIS BOOK

When the recipe says 1 cup all-purpose flour, this means 1 cup of flour measured without sifting. (Ignore the presifted label on flour sacks. Presifting can eliminate stones and foreign matter, but it cannot prevent the flour from compacting again en route to your grocer's shelf.) Measure the flour as follows. Loosen the flour in the sack or cannister with a spoon if it is compacted. Spoon the flour lightly into a 1-cup dry measure until it is heaped above the rim. Do not shake or tap the cup to settle the flour. Sweep a straight-edged knife or spatula across the rim of the cup to level the flour. A cup of unsifted all-purpose flour weighs 5 ounces. (A cup of unsifted cake flour weighs 4 ounces.)

If the recipe calls for 1 cup of sifted flour, the flour should be sifted before measuring as follows. Set the measuring cup on a sheet of wax paper. Sift the flour directly over the cup until it is heaped above the rim of the cup. Do not shake or tap the cup to settle the flour. Sweep a straight-edged knife or spatula across the rim of the cup to level the flour. A cup of sifted all-purpose flour weighs 4 ounces. (A cup of sifted cake flour weighs 3^1/$_2$ ounces.)

DRY AND LIQUID MEASURES

Dry measures refer to measuring cups designed to measure dry ingredients, not measuring cups that have been wiped dry. They are plastic or metal cups, which usually come in nested sets. Liquid measures refer to measuring cups designed to measure liquid ingredients. They are clear plastic or glass containers with a pouring spout and lines up the sides to indicate measurements.

When using dry measures, use the appropriate tools: a 1-cup measure to measure 1 cup, ^{1}/$_2$-cup measure to measure ^{1}/$_2$ cup, and so forth. Heap the dry ingredient above the rim, without packing it down. Do not tap or shake the cup to settle the ingredient. Sweep a straight-edged knife or spatula across the rim of the cup to level it.

When using liquid measures, set the measure on the counter; don't hold it up in the air. Pour liquid up to the appropriate mark and lower your head to read the measurement at eye level.

MELTING CHOCOLATE FOR RECIPES

Instructions for melting and handling chocolate are given in each recipe. Some points to remember:

Keep chocolate dry, unless otherwise directed in a recipe. Chocolate will not melt smoothly if it comes in contact with even small amounts of moisture. Thus, cutting boards, containers, and utensils that come in contact with chocolate should be kept dry. Avoid dripping or splashing water on the chocolate. (A larger quantity of liquid— at least 1 tablespoon for every 2 ounces of chocolate—*is* compatible with chocolate, however, which explains why some recipes call for chocolate and liquid melted together.)

If melted chocolate seizes (turns dull and lumpy and thick), moisture is probably the culprit. You may have to start over. However, unless the seized chocolate tastes burned, you may save it for a sauce (combined with hot cream) or make a cake or torte that calls for melting the chocolate with some butter.

Chocolate burns easily, especially when melted without other ingredients in the bowl. Milk chocolate and white chocolate are especially delicate. The object in melting chocolate is to transform it from solid to liquid, to make it warm, not hot. Chocolate is chopped so that it can be melted quickly and evenly, at a low temperature, without getting really hot. I usually chop dark chocolate into small to medium pieces and milk or white chocolate into very small pieces (like matchsticks or small peas). Chop chocolate on a cutting board with a large chef's knife or break it into bits with a multipronged ice/chocolate pick or chipper. Some people use a food processor. Melt chocolate uncovered. Melt in a microwave using Medium (50 percent) power for dark chocolate or Low (30 percent) power for milk or white. Or melt in the top of a double boiler over barely simmering water. Or melt chocolate in a heatproof bowl set directly in a skillet of barely simmering water. (If using the latter method for milk chocolate or white chocolate, turn the heat off under the skillet for 30 seconds before placing the bowl of chocolate in the water, then stir almost constantly.)

Whether you use the microwave, double boiler, or water bath, stir frequently to mix the warmest melted chocolate with the unmelted pieces. Remove the chocolate from the heat before the last pieces are melted, then stir until completely melted. Melted white and milk chocolate should feel barely warm when touched with your finger; darker chocolates should feel warm to very warm but not hot.

The same methods are used to melt chocolate together with butter and/or other ingredients, including sufficient liquid to prevent the chocolate from seizing. Hot liquid, such as cream, is sometimes poured over chopped chocolate, then stirred until the chocolate is completely melted and smooth. When this instruction is given, it is important that the chocolate be chopped finely enough to fully melt.

TO TEMPER CHOCOLATE, SEE PAGE 112.

MIXING IT UP

The secret to mixing each batter or dough properly is written into each recipe. Use the type of mixing utensil suggested in the recipe. Mixing with a spatula does not produce the same batter texture as mixing with a wire whisk, for example. Pay attention to whether mixing is described as folding, stirring, beating, or whisking, because it makes a difference. When a recipe calls for mixing (or folding or stirring, etc.) "just until the ingredient is incorporated," this means that extra mixing is discouraged; it may toughen the cake, deflate the batter, or cause other problems.

The order in which key ingredients are mixed can also be critical. Add and mix ingredients in the order the recipe calls for. If a recipe calls for stirring x into y, it is safe to assume that stirring y into x may not produce the same result.

In some recipes, flour and other dry ingredients are to be blended into the batter without excessive mixing. The trick? Follow the recipe: First whisk the flour thoroughly with the other dry ingredients (leavening, spices, salt, etc.) to distribute them evenly and to fluff and aerate the mixture. Then it will blend easily and thoroughly into batter or dough with very minimal mixing.

I prefer to turn the mixer off when I add flour to a dough or batter. Then I resume mixing on low speed. This works when the bowl is relatively tall—at least as tall as it is wide—and prevents the flour from flying out of the bowl when the mixer is turned on. Otherwise, while mixing at low speed, add the flour mixture gradually enough to keep it from flying out but without taking any more time than necessary.

CHILL OUT OR WARM UP?

The texture of cakes and other desserts can be *drastically* affected by the temperature of individual ingredients when they are mixed into the recipe. When a recipe calls for butter, milk, or eggs, or any other refrigerated ingredients at room temperature, this means 65° to 70°F., which is still cool (not warm) but not cold. Remove these items from the fridge early, or bring them to room temperature more quickly as follows:

• Put eggs (still in the shell) in a bowl of warm water, or crack and whisk them in a bowl set in a larger bowl of warm water.

• Microwave milk on Low (30 percent) power for just a few seconds, or set the measure into a bowl of hot water until no longer cold, but not warm.

• Cut butter into chunks and microwave very carefully, a few seconds at a time, on Low or Defrost, until pliable but not melted.

BAKING FOR BEST RESULTS

Preheating the oven means getting it up to temperature. This takes 15 to 20 minutes, depending on your oven. Something baked in the top of the oven will turn out different from the same thing baked in the bottom (remember that heat rises). I usually position a rack in the lower third of the oven so that a cake placed on the rack is actually just below center. When baking a sheet of cookies or something else very thin or shallow, I position the oven rack in the center. I also rotate cookie sheets and jelly-roll pans from back to front halfway through the baking.

COOLING

Unless otherwise instructed, cool baked items on a rack completely before covering or wrapping. Wrapping or covering warm baked goods results in damp, soggy textures and may encourage bacteria and/or mold.

CHOCOLATE NOTES

A Chocolate Note appears with the ingredients list in most recipes that call for bittersweet or semisweet chocolate. Consult it to have success using boutique or imported chocolates labeled by percentage rather than standard domestic semisweet or bittersweet chocolate. The Notes identify which chocolates fall within the range of the recipe, and they help you adjust recipes, if necessary, when using stronger chocolates. When there is no Chocolate Note in a recipe calling for bittersweet or semisweet chocolate, choose any favorite chocolate and proceed as directed.

For a more comprehensive treatment of chocolate percentages and more recipes using high-percentage chocolates, see my *BitterSweet: Recipes and Tales from a Life in Chocolate* (Artisan, 2003).

Fall chocolate begs to be woven into deep primal flavors and rich aromas: a harvest of nuts and lush fall fruit, the sweetness of caramel and honey. A generous double dose of chocolate ganache makes a heavenly marriage with layers of soft toasted hazelnut meringue in Mocha Marjolaine, and Chocolate Peanut Butter Layer Cake is hardly subtle. Chocolate also shines in a supporting role in myriad autumn desserts. I work it very carefully into the traditional repertoire to prevent upstaging or even ruining an already great dessert. Restraint is often my secret ingredient. Artfully added, chocolate brings new dimension to classics like pecan pie and spicy gingerbread. Chocolate Cranberry Bread Pudding is sure to create a brand-new holiday tradition. Fall chocolate is ripe with nuance and possibility.

chocolate peanut butter layer cake | An old favorite but with new accessories. Peanut brittle shards are like dramatic oversized jewels—gaudy but good. I use natural peanut butter.

FILLING

2/3 cup natural smooth peanut butter

1/4 teaspoon vanilla extract

1/3 cup powdered sugar, sifted after measuring

4 tablespoons (1/2 stick) unsalted butter, slightly softened

2 layers Chocolate Sour Cream Layer Cake (page 4), baked and cooled

FROSTING AND DECORATION

5 ounces bittersweet or semisweet chocolate, cut into small pieces

2/3 cup sour cream

4 to 6 ounces peanut brittle (see page 110) or a handful of salted or dry roasted peanuts

EQUIPMENT

8-inch round corrugated cardboard cake circle or cake pan bottom (optional)

CHOCOLATE NOTE

You can use any domestic semisweet or bittersweet chocolate without a percentage on the label, or any boutique or imported brand marked 50 to 60 percent. Or, substitute 4 1/2 ounces chocolate labeled 64 percent, or substitute 3 3/4 ounces chocolate labeled 66 to 72 percent and stir 1 tablespoon granulated sugar into the sour cream.

Beat the peanut butter, vanilla, powdered sugar, and butter just until blended and smooth. Turn 1 cake layer upside down on the cardboard circle or on a platter. Spread the peanut mixture evenly over the cake. Top with the second cake layer, right side up. Set aside.

Place the chocolate in a small bowl and set in a pan of barely simmering water. Stir frequently until melted and smooth. Or microwave on Medium (50 percent) power for 2 1/2 to 3 minutes, stirring from time to time. Off heat, scrape the sour cream on top of the chocolate and stir just to combine. Use immediately to frost the top and sides of the cake. If the frosting becomes too stiff to spread or loses its gloss, set the bowl in a pan of hot water for a few seconds to soften. Decorate the cake with peanuts or shards of peanut brittle. *Cake keeps at room temperature, in a covered container, for 2 to 3 days.*

chocolate sour cream layer cake

Start the autumn baking season with this versatile all-chocolate, all-purpose, American-style chocolate layer cake. I've updated it slightly so it's a little less sweet and more chocolatey and topped it with a tangy chocolate sour cream frosting that takes only minutes to make.

CAKE

1¼ cups all-purpose flour

⅔ cup unsweetened Dutch-process cocoa powder

⅜ teaspoon baking powder

⅜ teaspoon baking soda

½ teaspoon salt

½ cup sour cream or plain yogurt

16 tablespoons (2 sticks) unsalted butter, slightly softened

1¼ cups sugar

3 large eggs

1½ teaspoons vanilla extract

FROSTING

1 to 2 teaspoons powdered instant coffee (optional)

1½ teaspoons hot water (optional)

1 cup sour cream

8 ounces bittersweet or semisweet chocolate, cut into small pieces

EQUIPMENT

Two 8-inch round layer cake pans, lined on the bottom with a round of parchment paper and sprayed on the sides with vegetable oil spray or lightly greased

8-inch round corrugated cardboard cake circle or cake pan bottom (optional).

CHOCOLATE NOTE

You can use any domestic semisweet or bittersweet chocolate without a percentage on the label, or any boutique or imported brand marked 50 to 62 percent. Or, substitute 7 ounces chocolate labeled 64 percent, or substitute 6 ounces chocolate marked 66 to 72 percent and stir 4 teaspoons sugar into sour cream.

All ingredients should be at room temperature.

Position the rack in the lower third of the oven. Preheat the oven to 350°F.

Sift the flour, cocoa, baking powder, baking soda, and salt together 3 times. Set aside.

Combine the sour cream with ¼ cup water and set aside.

In a medium to large bowl with an electric mixer (using the flat beater or paddle instead of the whisk on heavy-duty stand mixers), beat the butter for a few seconds until creamy. Add the sugar in a steady stream and continue to beat (at high speed with a hand-held mixer or at medium speed with a stand mixer) until light and fluffy, about 4 minutes.

Meanwhile break the eggs into a cup, add the vanilla, and whisk to combine the whites and yolks. Beat the eggs into the butter mixture gradually, taking 1½ to 2 minutes, beating constantly.

Stop the mixer and add one third of the flour mixture to the bowl. Beat on low speed only until no flour is visible. Stop the mixer and add half of the sour cream. Beat only until blended. Repeat with half of the remaining flour mixture, then all of the remaining sour cream, and finally the remaining flour. Stop the mixer each time you add ingredients, then beat on low speed only enough to incorporate ingredients after each addition. Divide the batter between the prepared pans and spread evenly.

Bake until the cake starts to shrink away from the sides of the pan and a toothpick inserted in the center comes out clean, 25 to 30 minutes. Cool the cake in the pan on a rack for 5 to 10 minutes before unmolding. Invert each layer onto a rack and peel off the parchment liners. Turn the layers right side up and cool completely on the rack before assembling. *Cake can be prepared to this point, wrapped well, and kept at room temperature for 1 to 2 days before using, or frozen for up to 3 months.*

To make the frosting, dissolve the coffee powder, if using, in the hot water. Stir into the sour cream and set aside.

Place the chocolate in a small bowl and set in a pan of barely simmering water, stirring frequently until melted and smooth. Or microwave on Medium (50 percent) power for 3 to 4 minutes, stirring from time to time. Off heat, scrape the sour cream on top of the chocolate and stir to combine. Do not continue to stir after the mixture is combined and smooth. Use immediately. If the frosting becomes too stiff or loses its gloss, set the bowl in a pan of hot water for a few seconds to soften.

Turn 1 cooled cake layer upside down on a platter, if using, or corrugated cardboard. Spread about 2/3 cup of the frosting on top. Top with the second layer, right side up. Frost the top and sides with the remaining frosting. Store and serve at room temperature. *Cake keeps at room temperature, in a covered container, for 2 to 3 days.*

mocha marjolaine

A sophisticated fall birthday or celebration cake: four layers of soft nutty meringue filled with light mocha ganache and frosted with dark bittersweet ganache.

MERINGUE NUT LAYER	3/4 cup hazelnuts, toasted and completely cooled, skins rubbed off
	3/4 cup whole almonds, toasted and cooled
	1 1/2 tablespoons all-purpose flour
	3/4 cup sugar
	6 egg whites, at room temperature
	1/2 teaspoon cream of tartar
GANACHE	2 cups heavy cream
	13 ounces bittersweet or semisweet chocolate, finely chopped
	1 tablespoon plus 1 teaspoon instant espresso powder
DECORATION	Several caramel-glazed or gilded toasted hazelnuts (see page 110) and/or chocolate leaves (see page 109) (optional)
EQUIPMENT	16 x 12- or 17 x 11-inch jelly-roll pan, lined with parchment paper
CHOCOLATE NOTE	You can use any domestic bittersweet or semisweet chocolate without a percentage on the label, or any boutique or imported brand marked 50 to 60 percent. Or, substitute 11 ounces chocolate marked 60 to 64 percent, or substitute 9 1/2 ounces chocolate marked 66 to 72 percent and dissolve 4 or 5 teaspoons sugar in the hot cream before adding it to the chocolate.

Position a rack in the center of the oven. Preheat the oven to 325°F. In a food processor with a clean, dry bowl, pulse the hazelnuts, almonds, flour, and 1/2 cup of the sugar to a fine meal. Set aside.

To make the meringue layers, in a large, clean, dry mixer bowl, combine the egg whites with the cream of tartar. Beat at medium speed until soft peaks form when the beaters are lifted. On high speed, gradually beat in the remaining 1/4 cup sugar until the egg whites are stiff but not dry. Pour the nuts over the egg whites and fold with a rubber spatula just until incorporated. Spread the batter evenly in the lined pan.

Bake until golden brown and springy to the touch, 25 to 30 minutes. Cool in the pan set on a rack. *The meringue layer may be prepared up to 2 days ahead. Cover tightly but carefully and store at room temperature.*

To make the ganache filling and glaze, bring 1 1/3 cups of the cream to a simmer. Off heat, stir in the chocolate until it is completely melted and smooth. Transfer 1 cup of the ganache to another bowl. Stir in the espresso powder and the remaining 2/3 cup of cold cream to make a lighter ganache. Chill the light ganache for at least 2 hours or until needed. Leave the dark ganache at room temperature to cool and thicken.

To assemble the cake, cut around the edges of the pan to detach the meringue. Invert the pan over a sheet of wax paper and remove the pan. Peel off the paper liner and cut the meringue in half crosswise, then in half lengthwise, to make 4 rectangular layers.

Use a pancake turner to set 1 layer of meringue on a baking sheet. Remove the chilled ganache from the refrigerator and beat it with a hand-held mixer until it is light colored and stiff enough to hold good shape for spreading. Spread one third of the ganache evenly over the layer. Place a second layer on top and press it level. Repeat with half of the remaining ganache and the third layer. Finally, spread the remaining ganache and top with the last layer. Refrigerate the cake until firm, at least 1 hour.

Remove the cake from the refrigerator. Using a sharp serrated knife and a gentle sawing motion, trim the sides of the cake evenly. Spread the top and sides of the cake with a very thin coat of dark ganache just to create a smooth surface. If the ganache is stiff or dull, set the bowl in another bowl of hot water and stir until it is soft, shiny, and spreadable. (If the glaze is not smooth, adjust the consistency by adding a tablespoon or more of cream, milk, or water.) Frost the top and sides of the cake with smooth or swirly strokes. Decorate, if desired, with gilded nuts and/or chocolate leaves. Slide a spatula under the cake to transfer it to a serving dish. Refrigerate to store. Remove the cake from the refrigerator 30 to 60 minutes before serving to soften the layers and open up the flavors.

honey-drizzled chocolate cheese fritters

These delightful fritters were adapted from a recipe by Marcella Hazan. They are perfect for Rosh Hashanah (because of the honey) or Hanukkah (because they are fried). Regardless of symbolism, they are too good and too simple to save just for a holiday. Try maple syrup in lieu of honey once in a while.

15 ounces ricotta cheese

3 eggs

1/2 cup all-purpose flour

2 tablespoons melted butter

1 1/2 teaspoons grated orange zest

1/8 teaspoon salt

1 1/2 ounces semisweet chocolate, finely chopped

Vegetable oil, for frying

3/4 cup honey, warm

EQUIPMENT   Wide skillet

Mix the ricotta and eggs with a fork. Add the flour and mix just until incorporated. Add the butter, orange zest, salt, and chocolate and stir just until thoroughly combined. *Batter may be prepared to this point, covered, and refrigerated up to 2 days in advance.*

Either fry fritters up to 2 hours in advance of serving and serve them at room temperature (they are delicious), or fry and serve them hot or warm. Do not keep fritters in a warm oven for long or they will dry and toughen. Just before serving time, or up to 2 hours before, place a small ovenproof platter lined with several layers of paper towel or a cloth napkin in a 200°F. oven.

In a wide skillet, heat 1/2 inch of oil over medium heat until a few drops of batter sizzle vigorously when added to the pan. Carefully add rounded tablespoonfuls of batter to the hot oil. Do not crowd the fritters; they need space to fry properly and to turn. Fry until brown on 1 side, then turn and fry the other side until brown. Transfer the fritters to a warm platter with a fork or tongs. Repeat until all the batter is fried. Serve drizzled with warm honey, or pass the honey separately.

honey walnut tart

Usher in a rich, sweet New Year with this divine double-crust (and conveniently do-ahead) Swiss classic. Thin slices are perfect finger food for a holiday sweet table on any occasion from Rosh Hashanah straight through New Year's Day. Without the glaze, the tart is delicious too, though less dressy—just serve it right side up rather than inverted.

CRUST

10 tablespoons (1¼ sticks) melted unsalted butter

1½ tablespoons sugar

¼ teaspoon salt

½ teaspoon vanilla extract

Grated zest of ½ small lemon (optional)

1 egg

2 cups all-purpose flour

FILLING

1 cup sugar

⅓ cup honey

2 tablespoons light corn syrup

½ teaspoon lemon juice

⅛ teaspoon salt

1 cup heavy cream

3 tablespoons unsalted butter, cut into chunks

1½ teaspoons vanilla extract

2¾ cups broken or very coarsely chopped walnuts

GLAZE

6 ounces bittersweet or semisweet chocolate, coarsely chopped

8 tablespoons (1 stick) unsalted butter

1 tablespoon honey

16 plain or caramel-glazed walnut halves (see page 110) and/or gold leaf (page 109)

EQUIPMENT

9½-inch tart pan with removable bottom

Long-handled silicone spatula or wooden spoon

Candy thermometer

To make the tart pastry and line the pan, in a medium bowl whisk the melted butter with the sugar, salt, 1½ teaspoons water, vanilla, lemon zest, and egg. Stir in the flour just until it is completely moistened. The dough should not be smooth. Divide the dough into 2 unequal pieces (about 60–40). Roll the smaller piece between 2 pieces of wax paper to a circle about 10 inches in diameter and ⅛ inch thick. Without removing the wax paper, slide the circle onto a cookie sheet and refrigerate. Press the remaining dough evenly across the bottom and up the sides of the tart pan, pinching it to extend ½ inch above the rim of the pan. Refrigerate until needed.

To make the filling, combine the sugar, honey, corn syrup, lemon juice, and salt in a 1½- to 2-quart heavy-bottomed saucepan. Cook over medium heat, stirring gently with a silicone spatula or wooden spoon, until the mixture is liquefied and begins to simmer around the edges. Wash the sugar and syrup from the sides of the pot with a wet pastry brush or wad of paper towel. Cover and continue to cook about 3 minutes. Meanwhile, rinse the sugar crystals from the spatula or spoon before using it again later. Uncover the pot and wash the sides again. Insert a candy thermometer without letting it touch the bottom of the pot. Cook, uncovered, without stirring, until the mixture reaches 305°F. Meanwhile heat the cream to a simmer. Turn off the heat and keep the hot cream handy.

continued

HONEY WALNUT
TART

As soon as the sugar mixture reaches 305°F., turn the heat off. Immediately stir in the butter chunks. Gradually stir in the hot cream; it will bubble up and steam dramatically, so be careful. Turn the heat on and adjust it so that the mixture boils energetically but not violently. Stir until any thickened syrup at the bottom of the pot is dissolved and the mixture is smooth. Continue to cook, stirring occasionally, until the thermometer registers 246°F. When the syrup is done, remove the pot from the heat. Stir in the vanilla and walnuts.

Position a rack in the lower third of the oven. Preheat the oven to 425°F.

To bake the tart, remove the tart pan from the refrigerator. Pour in the warm filling and spread it evenly. Wait 1 or 2 minutes for the pastry to soften so you can fold it, without cracking, over the filling around the edge of the tart. Moisten the folded pastry with water. Remove the pastry circle from the refrigerator and peel off the top sheet of paper. Cut two 5-inch gashes in the center of the pastry to form an x. Lift the edges of the paper and invert the pastry over the tart. Press well to seal the pastry at the edges and trim the excess against the rim of the pan. Remove the paper and trimmings.

Set the pan on a baking sheet and bake 20 minutes. If the pastry is beginning to brown, lay a sheet of foil on top. Bake 10 to 15 minutes more, to be sure the bottom crust is cooked and the top is deep golden brown. Cool the tart in the pan on a rack. If filling has leaked at the edges, remove the rim of the pan while the tart is still hot, to avoid sticking. Cool at least 4 hours or overnight.

Invert the cooled tart on a plate and remove the rim and pan bottom. Leave the tart upside down. Slide the pan bottom beneath the tart for support.

To glaze the tart, in the top of a double boiler or in a heatproof bowl set in a pan of barely simmering water, melt the chocolate with the butter and honey, stirring frequently, until smooth. Cool the glaze to 90°F.

Pour the glaze over the tart and spread it with a metal spatula. Let the glaze harden at room temperature. Decorate with walnut halves and/or flecks of gold leaf. Store and serve at room temperature, cut into 16 thin or about 24 extra-thin slices. *The tart keeps well (some say it improves with age) for at least 1 week at room temperature.*

chocolate cranberry bread pudding | My family is passionate
about Thanksgiving. Our custom of eating desserts for breakfast for
as many days as possible requires the production of three times
the number of pies or puddings needed for the Big Meal. Desserts
must be divine, but not so rich that the sated cannot partake after
a sumptuous dinner, and must pass the breakfast test, too. Apple
pie is obvious, but I wanted something chocolate.

1 loaf (16 ounces) challah or brioche

8 tablespoons (1 stick) melted unsalted butter

2 cups fresh or dried cranberries

1²/₃ cups milk

1 cup heavy cream

Scant cup sugar

14 ounces bittersweet or semisweet chocolate, chopped

7 eggs

1 teaspoon vanilla extract

Lightly sweetened whipped cream or crème fraîche (optional)

EQUIPMENT 13x9-inch glass or earthenware baking dish or two 9-inch glass pie pans, buttered

CHOCOLATE NOTE You can use any domestic bittersweet or semisweet chocolate without a percentage on the label, or any boutique or imported brand marked 50 to 62 percent. Or, substitute 10 ounces chocolate marked 66 to 72 percent and increase sugar by 2 tablespoons.

Position the rack in the lower third of the oven. Preheat the oven to 350°F.

Tear the loaf into large shreds, about 2 x ³/₄ inches. To do this, pinch a piece of the bread at the top of the loaf and start pulling. If the loaf is sliced, tear the slices. Spread the shreds on a large baking sheet and bake until lightly toasted, about 5 minutes. Remove from the oven and immediately drizzle melted butter over the bread. Toss lightly to distribute the butter. Cover the bottom of the pan or pans with half of the bread. Sprinkle all the cranberries over the bread. Top with the remaining bread. Set aside.

In a heavy saucepan, heat the milk, cream, and sugar to a simmer. Off heat, add the chocolate and stir until melted and smooth. In a medium bowl, whisk the eggs and vanilla. Add the chocolate mixture to the eggs and stir until well blended. Pour the mixture over the bread, making sure the top layer of bread is completely moistened. Cover the pan loosely with a piece of foil.

Bake for 15 minutes. Remove the foil and bake 15 minutes more, or until the pudding bubbles vigorously around the edges although the center is still very liquid if the pan is jiggled. Remove the pudding from the oven (it will continue to thicken) and cool on a rack. Serve warm, at room temperature, or cold, plain or with a dab of whipped cream or crème fraîche.

ripe figs with mint ganache

Toss out any preconceived notion you may have about mint-flavored chocolate and prepare for a revelation. Select excellent chocolate and fresh peppermint with bright green leaves rather than the dark-edged spearmint. This simple but sophisticated dessert is equally at home in rustic earthenware bowls or your best stemmed crystal.

1 bunch fresh peppermint

1 cup heavy cream

6 ounces bittersweet or semisweet chocolate, finely chopped

12 ripe flavorful figs, cut into halves or quarters

1 cup or 1/2 pint fresh raspberries (optional)

1/3 cup slivered or sliced almonds, toasted and cooled

CHOCOLATE NOTE   You can use any domestic bittersweet or semisweet chocolate without a percentage on the label, or any boutique or imported brand marked 50 to 62 percent. Higher-percentage chocolates will require some or all of the extra cream to make a smooth fluid sauce, and you can adjust sweetness with sugar, if desired.

Rinse the mint and blot it dry with paper towels. Set aside 6 to 8 good-looking small sprigs for garnish. Chop enough of the remaining mint leaves to make 1/3 cup (lightly packed). Combine the chopped mint and 3/4 cup of the cream in a small saucepan and bring it to a boil. Remove the pan from the heat. Cover and let steep for 5 minutes.

Meanwhile, place the chocolate in a medium bowl and set a strainer over it. Pour the cream through the strainer, pressing gently on the mint to extract the cream. Discard the mint. Stir the chocolate mixture gently until it is perfectly smooth and all of the chocolate is melted. (If the sauce is too thick or if it isn't smooth, add more cream as necessary.) Cool the chocolate mixture to the consistency of a thick

sauce (or cool it completely and rewarm it very gently in a pan of barely simmering water when ready to serve).

Cut the figs into quarters. For each serving, spoon about 2 tablespoons of sauce into a shallow bowl or compote dish. Scatter 6 to 8 fig quarters and some raspberries, if desired, over the sauce. Drizzle a little extra sauce over the fruit, if desired. Sprinkle with toasted almonds. Garnish with a sprig of mint.

Stuffed Figs: Cut the figs into halves. Cool the ganache to a soft, spreadable consistency. Spread a mound of ganache on the cut surface of each fig and sprinkle with toasted almonds.

gingerbread with milk chocolate chunks

The cake itself is a bolt of pure ginger heat, softened with honey, then made richer and somehow even more exotic with the addition of milk chocolate. Even if you normally prefer semisweet or bittersweet chocolate, trust me on this one. To a sweet New Year!

1 1/2 cups all-purpose flour

1/4 teaspoon salt

1 teaspoon soda

1/4 cup (packed) light brown sugar

1/4 cup light unsulfured molasses

1/4 cup honey

1 egg

1/2 cup very finely minced peeled ginger

6 tablespoons (3/4 stick) unsalted butter, cut into pieces

4 ounces milk chocolate, chopped into small pieces, or milk chocolate chips

Whipped cream or crème fraîche (optional)

EQUIPMENT   9-inch square or 9-inch round pan, lined with parchment paper or greased

Position a rack in the lower third of the oven. Preheat the oven to 350°F.

In a medium bowl, whisk together the flour, salt, and soda. Set aside.

In a large bowl, combine the brown sugar, molasses, and honey. Whisk in the egg and ginger. In a saucepan, heat the butter and 1/2 cup water until the butter is melted. Whisk the hot mixture into the honey mixture. Add the flour mixture and stir until smooth. Stir in the chocolate. Scrape the batter into the pan.

Bake until a toothpick inserted in the center of the cake comes out clean, except (possibly) for the melted chocolate, 25 to 30 minutes for a square cake, a little longer for the round. Cool the cake on a rack. Invert the cake, remove the pan, and peel off the paper liner. Serve right side up, warm or at room temperature, plain or with a dab of whipped cream or crème fraîche.

chocolate pecan pie | SERVES 8 TO 10

This mahogany-hued pie bursts with pecans, brown sugar, and rum with a perfectly balanced infusion of dark chocolate. My friend cookbook author Stephen Schmidt taught me to heat the filling before pouring it into a hot prebaked piecrust for extra rich flavor—and to banish the traditional soggy piecrust forever. This pie is a triumph.

CRUST

1 1/2 cups all-purpose flour

3/4 teaspoon salt

10 tablespoons (1 1/4 sticks) unsalted butter

FILLING

2 ounces bittersweet or semisweet chocolate, coarsely chopped

1/4 cup light corn syrup

1 tablespoon melted butter

1 cup (lightly packed) dark brown sugar

1/4 teaspoon salt

1 tablespoon rum, bourbon, or brandy

1 teaspoon vanilla extract

3 eggs

2 cups pecan halves, toasted

Lightly sweetened whipped cream

EQUIPMENT

9-inch glass pie pan, not a deep-dish pan

CHOCOLATE NOTE

You can use any domestic bittersweet or semisweet chocolate without a percentage on the label, or any boutique or imported brand marked 50 to 62 percent. Or, substitute 1 1/2 ounces chocolate marked 70 percent, or 1 ounce unsweetened chocolate.

To make the crust, in a large mixing bowl, thoroughly mix the flour and salt. Cut the butter into chunks and add it to the bowl. Cut the butter into successively smaller pieces with 2 knives or a pastry blender, scraping the bottom of the bowl and tossing the pieces to coat and separate them with flour as you work. Continue until the largest pieces of butter are the size of peas and the rest resemble bread crumbs. Do not allow the butter to melt or form a paste with the flour. Drizzle 4 tablespoons of water over the flour mixture. Mix with a rubber spatula or a fork, folding and pressing the dough to distribute the moisture. If the dough seems too dry, drizzle in 1 tablespoon more water until the dough is just moist enough to hold together when pressed with the flat of the spatula or fork. Use your hands to press the dough into a flat disk, pressing in any loose pieces. Wrap and refrigerate for 30 minutes or up to 3 days before use.

Remove the dough from the refrigerator and let it stand until it is pliable enough to roll without cracking. On a lightly floured surface, roll the dough into a circle about 1/8 inch thick, stopping from time to time to rotate the dough and dust the surface as necessary, to keep it from sticking. Dust excess flour from the rolled-out circle. Fold the dough into quarters. Transfer it to the pie pan and unfold, easing the pastry into the pan without stretching. Trim the dough about 1 inch beyond the rim of the pan. Turn excess dough under and flute or crimp the edge. Refrigerate at least 30 minutes before baking. Reserve a few dough scraps for patching later, if necessary.

Position a rack in the lower third of the oven. Preheat the oven to 400°F.

Remove chilled piecrust from the refrigerator. Tear off a square of wide foil (or fold 2 pieces together to make the width) and press it, shiny side down, across the bottom and up the sides of the crust. Arrange the excess foil over (but not touching) the edges of the crust, like an awning, to prevent early browning. With a fork, prick the bottom of the crust all over, piercing right through the foil. Fill the foil-lined crust with dried beans or pie weights. Bake the weighted crust for 20 minutes. Remove the foil liner and pie weights. Bake 10 to 12 minutes more, or until the bottom of the crust is golden brown.

To make the filling (do this while the crust is baking), in the top of a double boiler over barely simmering water (or in a heatproof bowl set in a skillet of barely simmering water), combine the chocolate with the corn syrup and butter. Stir until the chocolate is completely melted and smooth. Stir in the brown sugar,

salt, rum, and vanilla. Add the eggs, stirring until the mixture is well blended and hot to the touch. Set aside the entire double boiler, stirring the filling from time to time, until needed.

When the crust is ready, remove it from the oven, but leave the oven on. Use reserved dough scraps if necessary to patch any holes. Pour the pecans into the crust. Pour the hot filling over the nuts and return the pie to the oven. Bake until the filling is puffed and cracked at the edges and brown in patches but still jiggles in the center when nudged, 10 to 12 minutes. A knife inserted in the pie will not come out clean; it will still be very gooey. If the edges of the crust are browning too fast before the pie is done, cover with a 12-inch square of foil with a 7-inch circle cut out from the center. Cool the pie on a rack. Serve warm or at room temperature with lightly sweetened whipped cream.

Photograph on page 20

maya's day of the dead cookies | Here's a whimsical and witty twist on the old black-and-white cookie. My friend and assistant, Maya Klein, invented this clever, slice-and-bake method to conjure up a host of creepy-looking skulls with hollow eye sockets and evil grins. Lots of fun in honor of this ancient Mexican ritual, which occurs every year around All Souls' Day.

VANILLA DOUGH

2 cups all-purpose flour

1/2 teaspoon baking powder

1/4 teaspoon salt

8 tablespoons (1 stick) unsalted butter, softened

1 cup sugar

1 egg

1 1/2 teaspoons vanilla extract

CHOCOLATE DOUGH

1 cup all-purpose flour

1/2 cup unsweetened cocoa powder, Dutch process or natural

1/2 teaspoon baking soda

1/4 teaspoon baking powder

1/8 teaspoon salt

8 tablespoons (1 stick) unsalted butter, softened

1/2 cup (packed) brown sugar, lump free

1/2 cup granulated sugar

1 egg

1 teaspoon vanilla extract

EQUIPMENT

Baking sheets lined with parchment paper

To make the vanilla dough, mix the flour, baking powder, and salt together thoroughly with a whisk or a fork. Set aside.

In a large mixing bowl, beat the butter and sugar with an electric mixer until light and fluffy, 3 to 4 minutes. Beat in the egg and vanilla. On low speed, beat in the flour just until incorporated. Form the dough into a log about 2 inches in diameter. Set aside.

To make the chocolate dough, in a medium bowl, mix the flour, cocoa, baking soda, baking powder, and salt together thoroughly with a whisk or fork. Set aside.

In a large mixing bowl, beat the butter, brown sugar, and granulated sugar with the back of a spoon or an electric mixer until smooth and creamy but not fluffy (less than 1 1/2 minutes with an electric mixer). Beat in the egg and vanilla. On low speed, beat in the flour mixture and mix just until incorporated. Form dough into a log the same length as the vanilla log. If the dough is too soft and sticky to handle, place it in the freezer to firm up.

To shape the skulls, reshape each log of dough so that it is skull-shaped rather than round: Make one side of "the skull" narrow for the chin and jaw and leave the other side wide for the cranium. Wrap and refrigerate the chocolate dough. Form features in the vanilla dough, using the handle of a wooden spoon to poke holes for eyes through the entire length of the log. Form the nose with a skewer, poking two holes for nostrils. Form the mouth by inserting a narrow table knife and wiggling it back and forth gently to lengthen and widen the opening. Don't try for perfection: irregular holes make the best and weirdest skulls. Wrap and refrigerate the vanilla dough. Chill both doughs at least 2 hours, preferably overnight.

Position racks in the upper and lower thirds of the oven. Preheat the oven to 350°F. Cut the chocolate dough into 1/8-inch slices and place them at least 1 1/2 inches apart on the lined baking sheets. Cut the vanilla dough into 1/8-inch slices and place 1 slice on top of each chocolate slice. Bake until pale golden at the edges, 12 minutes, rotating the baking sheets from top to bottom and front to back halfway through the baking. Slide parchment liners onto cooling racks or transfer the cookies directly from the baking sheets to the rack with a metal pancake turner, waiting 1 or 2 minutes if necessary to let the cookies firm up before moving them. Cool cookies completely before stacking or storing. *Cookies keep at least 1 week in an airtight container.*

Photograph on page 21

chocolate-dipped caramel apples

Don't wait for Halloween to double dip the season's best apples in vanilla caramel and your favorite chocolate. These make pretty and delicious gifts. Make the full batch of caramel even if you want to dip only eight apples. Leftover caramel keeps for ages. Simply reheat to dip more apples or dilute with cream to make caramel sauce.

2 cups sugar

3/4 cup light corn syrup

1/4 cup honey

1/4 teaspoon salt

2 cups heavy cream

3 tablespoons unsalted butter, cut into chunks

1 tablespoon plus 1 teaspoon vanilla extract

Up to 16 small to medium apples, cold

1 1/4 pounds chocolate

5 to 6 ounces chopped toasted nuts (optional)

EQUIPMENT

Long-handled silicone spatula or wooden spoon

Candy thermometer

Up to 16 Popsicle sticks

Combine the sugar, corn syrup, honey, and salt in a heavy-bottomed 3-quart saucepan. Cook over medium heat, stirring with a spatula or spoon, until the mixture begins to simmer around the edges. Wash the sugar and syrup from the inside of the pot with a wet pastry brush or a wad of paper towel dipped in water. Cover and continue to cook for about 3 minutes. Meanwhile rinse the spatula or spoon before using it again later. Uncover the pot and wash the sides once more. Insert a candy thermometer without letting it touch the bottom of the pot. Cook, uncovered, without stirring, until the mixture reaches 305°F., 5 to 10 minutes. Meanwhile bring the cream to a simmer and keep it hot until needed.

When the sugar mixture reaches 305°F., turn the heat off. Stir in the butter chunks. Gradually stir in the hot cream; it will bubble up and steam dramatically, so be careful. Turn the heat back on under the pot so that the mixture boils energetically but not violently. Continue to cook, stirring occasionally, until the temperature reaches 250°F., about 30 minutes. Remove the pot from the heat. Stir in the vanilla. Transfer the caramel to a smaller pot or heatproof bowl deep enough to dip the apples. Cool for 10 minutes.

Impale each apple on a stick. Holding the stick, dip an apple into the caramel, allowing the excess to flow back into the pot. Set the apple on a sheet of wax paper. If the caramel gets too cool it will slide entirely off of the apples! If necessary, reheat gently (without simmering), then continue to dip. Repeat to coat each apple. Let the dipped apples set until caramel is cool and firm, at least 30 minutes.

Following the instructions on page 112, melt and temper the chocolate. Or simply melt (without tempering) 1 pound of chocolate. Dip each apple into the chocolate, allowing excess chocolate to flow back into the bowl. Sprinkle with nuts, if desired. Set the dipped apples on a tray lined with wax paper. Apples coated with untempered chocolate must be refrigerated to prevent discoloration. Apples coated with tempered chocolate may be kept at room temperature.

winter

Cold weather is an easy excuse to revel in pure unadulterated chocolate, the more intense the better. Chocolate is a warm reward when it's freezing cold outside, a centerpiece of celebrations, a gracious gift, or a romantic offering. I set subtlety aside in this season in favor of excess. I want my chocolate ultra rich, dense, dark, and dramatic. I'll have it stark naked or accentuated with a splash of raspberry, a slather of cream, or a shot of whiskey. Bittersweet memories are made of this. Chocolate truffles, chocolate soufflés, and flourless chocolate cake celebrate chocolate in its purest form. Winter chocolate is a force of nature.

chocolate banana blintzes

This is a great party dessert. The blintzes look complicated (which they aren't) and fancy (which they are). Simple do-ahead steps can be completed a day or more in advance. A few minutes of your attention at serving time are amply rewarded when the first fork breaks a tender crepe bursting with bananas and warm chocolate sauce.

CREPES

3 eggs

1 cup all-purpose flour

1/8 teaspoon salt

1 3/4 cups milk

2 tablespoons melted butter

Butter or oil, for frying

SAUCE

7 ounces bittersweet or semisweet chocolate, chopped into small pieces

1/2 cup milk, plus extra if needed

2 teaspoons sugar

1/2 teaspoon vanilla extract

3 large ripe bananas

Butter, for frying

Sour cream, for serving (optional)

EQUIPMENT

6-inch frying pan

Tray, lined with wax paper

CHOCOLATE NOTE You can use any domestic bittersweet or semisweet chocolate without a percentage on the label, or any boutique or imported brand labeled 50 to 60 percent. Higher-percentage chocolates will require extra milk to make the sauce smooth and fluid. You can adjust sweetness by adding sugar to taste.

To make crepes, combine eggs, flour, salt, milk, and melted butter in a blender or food processor. Pulse just until blended. Chill for 1 hour or up to 1 day.

Heat a 6-inch frying pan over medium-high heat. Brush it lightly with butter. Pour in 2 tablespoons of batter and tilt the pan immediately to coat the surface evenly. When the crepe is uniformly translucent and the surface no longer looks wet, 45 seconds to 1 minute, loosen the edges with a spatula and invert the pan over a piece of wax paper. Repeat with the remaining batter, buttering the pan when necessary. *Use the crepes immediately, or stack between sheets of wax paper, cover airtight, and refrigerate up to 2 days.*

To make the sauce, mix chocolate, milk, sugar, and vanilla in the top of a double boiler over barely simmering water. Or microwave on Medium (50 percent) power, about 2 minutes. Stir frequently until smooth, adding milk as necessary. Use the warm sauce immediately or set aside and use cool. *The sauce keeps several days in the refrigerator. Rewarm gently before use.*

To assemble the blintzes, slice the bananas 1/4 inch thick. Place 3 slices in a row, horizontally, in the middle of a crepe. Spread 1 tablespoon of sauce over them. Fold 2 sides of the crepe, then the top, over the bananas. Fold the bottom up to overlap. Place on a tray. Cover with plastic wrap and refrigerate at least 1 hour or up to 2 days.

To serve, heat a large frying pan over medium-high heat. When the pan is hot, add 1 tablespoon of butter and swirl to coat the pan. Cook as many blintzes as will fit comfortably until just browned, about 30 seconds, on each side. Serve plain or with sour cream, if desired.

winter solstice cookies

Let the sun shine through the translucent amber caramels of these fine crunchy chocolate cookies. They make pretty Christmas tree ornaments as well.

1 cup all-purpose flour

¹/₂ cup unsweetened cocoa powder, Dutch process or natural

¹/₂ teaspoon baking soda

¹/₄ teaspoon baking powder

¹/₈ teaspoon salt

8 tablespoons (1 stick) unsalted butter, softened

¹/₂ cup (packed) brown sugar, lump free

¹/₂ cup granulated sugar

1 egg

1 teaspoon vanilla extract

Basic Caramel (page 111)

EQUIPMENT

Cookie sheets, lined with parchment paper or foil
1-inch round cookie cutter

To make the cookies, in a medium bowl, mix the flour, cocoa, baking soda, baking powder, and salt together thoroughly with a whisk or fork. Set aside.

In a large mixing bowl, beat the butter, brown sugar, and granulated sugar with the back of a spoon or a mixer until smooth and creamy but not fluffy (less than 1¹/₂ minutes with an electric mixer). Mix in the egg and vanilla. Add the flour mixture and mix just until incorporated. Form the dough into a log about 6 inches long and 2¹/₂ inches in diameter. Chill for at least 3 hours, preferably overnight.

Position the racks in the upper and lower thirds of the oven. Preheat the oven to 350°F.

Using a sharp knife, cut the log into slices ¹/₄ inch thick. Place the slices 1¹/₂ inches apart on the lined cookie sheets. Bake until the cookies have puffed up and settled down again, rotating the cookie sheets from top to bottom and front to back halfway through the baking, 10 to 12 minutes.

Do not detach the cookies. Cool for 3 to 5 minutes, then cut and remove a 1-inch circle from the center of each one. Slide the parchment onto cooling racks or set the cookie sheet itself on a rack to cool completely. Transfer cooled cookies to a clean sheet of parchment paper.

Make the caramel, and immediately plunge the saucepan into a pan of ice water for 20 seconds to stop the cooking. Spoon a little caramel carefully into the center of each cookie. Set aside to cool and harden. Store cookies airtight.

chocolate latkes

There are no potatoes or added fat in these! Lots of chocolate and coconut make for a crunchy and chewy exterior and a wonderfully brownielike interior. Besides for Hanukkah, you can also bake the latkes for Passover—just call them Chocolate Coconut Macaroons!

4 egg whites

3 cups sweetened shredded coconut

3¹/₂ ounces semisweet or bittersweet chocolate, finely chopped

6 tablespoons sugar

2 teaspoons vanilla extract

Scant ¹/₄ teaspoon salt

EQUIPMENT   2 cookie sheets, lined with parchment paper or foil

Position racks in the upper and lower thirds of the oven. Preheat the oven to 350°F.

To make the latkes, combine all of the ingredients in a large heatproof mixing bowl, preferably stainless steel (the ingredients heat up faster in stainless steel than in glass). Set the bowl in a skillet of barely simmering water and stir the mixture, scraping the bottom to prevent burning, until it is sticky and hot to the touch.

Scoop rounded tablespoons of the mixture about 2 inches apart on the cookie sheets. Flatten each cookie slightly with your fingers to resemble miniature potato pancakes. Bake until the cookies feel dry on the surface and the edges and the protruding coconut shreds are dark golden brown (despite the chocolate color) and the interior still looks like melted chocolate, 13 to 15 minutes. Rotate the sheets from front to back and upper to lower about halfway through. Slide the parchment onto a cooling rack. Cool the cookies completely before removing them from the parchment.

The cookies are most delicious on the day they are baked—the exterior is crisp and chewy and the interior soft and moist. Cookies may be stored, airtight, for 4 to 5 days.

chocolate cream puffs with spun sugar

For Christmas or New Year's Eve, I deconstruct the traditional croquembouche (omitting its precarious architecture) and fill crisp caramel-glazed puffs with chocolate rum custard. It's still a little involved, but wildly worth the effort. Spun sugar is far easier than it looks, and your guests will love watching you do it.

CHOCOLATE RUM CUSTARD

6 ounces bittersweet or semisweet chocolate, finely chopped

2 teaspoons vanilla extract

3 tablespoons rum

4¹/₂ tablespoons sugar

2 tablespoons all-purpose flour

2 tablespoons cornstarch

4 egg yolks

1¹/₂ cups milk

PUFFS

4 tablespoons (¹/₂ stick) unsalted butter, cut into 8 pieces

2 teaspoons sugar

¹/₈ teaspoon salt

3 tablespoons milk

¹/₂ cup all-purpose flour, sifted after measuring

3 eggs, lightly whisked

1 cup sugar, for glaze and spun sugar

EQUIPMENT

Heavy cookie sheet or sheets, greased and floured

Pastry bag

Plain pastry tip with a ⁷/₁₆-inch opening (Ateco #805) and a star tip (Ateco #823 or #824)

To make the custard, place the chocolate, vanilla, and rum in a medium bowl. Set aside. In another medium bowl, combine the sugar, flour, and cornstarch. Add the egg yolks and beat with a hand-held mixer until the mixture is pale and thick, 1 to 2 minutes. Set aside.

Heat the milk in a small nonreactive saucepan until it forms a skin. Pour the hot milk gradually over the yolk mixture, whisking constantly until all of the milk is added. Return the mixture to the saucepan and cook on medium heat, stirring constantly with a wire whisk, reaching all over the bottom and sides of the pan, until the custard thickens considerably. Continue to cook and whisk for 1¹/₂ minutes more. Scrape the custard on top of the chocolate. Stir until the chocolate is melted and completely combined with the custard. Cover the surface of the custard with plastic wrap and refrigerate until needed. *Custard may be kept refrigerated for 2 to 3 days.*

Position a rack in the lower third of the oven. Preheat the oven to 400°F.

To make puffs, combine the butter, sugar, and salt with the milk and ¹/₃ cup water in a 1¹/₂- to 2-quart heavy-bottomed saucepan. Bring to a boil over medium heat, stirring occasionally, so that the butter is completely melted by the time the mixture boils. Remove the pot from the stove and pour in the flour all at once; stir with a wooden spoon to form a thick paste. Over, medium heat, dry the paste slightly by stirring and pushing it all over the sides and bottom of the pot until the pot looks clean but coated with a buttery film.

Transfer the hot paste to the bowl of an electric mixer or a bowl in which you can operate a hand-held mixer. Mix for 1 minute to cool slightly. Pour about 2 tablespoons of the egg into the paste and mix until incorporated. Gradually, in 3 or 4 additions, add nearly all of the rest of the egg, beating well after each addition until the eggs are absorbed and the paste is smooth, very thick and shiny, and falls slowly from a wooden spoon. Add the remaining egg judiciously, only if the paste seems too thick.

Fit the pastry bag with the plain tip and fill it with warm paste. Pipe mounds a scant 1 1/2 inches in diameter and 1/2 to 5/8 inch tall, about 1 1/2 inches apart, on the cookie sheet or sheets. Brush gently with water. Place a pan of hot tap water on the floor of the oven.

Bake, 1 sheet at a time, until the pastries are puffed and golden brown, 18 to 20 minutes. Turn the oven temperature down to 375°F. Remove the pan of water. Stab the sides of each pastry with a sharp knife to release steam. Bake 5 to 10 minutes more. Turn the oven off and leave the pastries inside 5 minutes more. Remove and cool puffs on a rack. *Cooled puffs may be stored in an airtight container in the refrigerator up to 3 days or frozen up to 1 month. Recrisp the pastries in a 400°F. oven for a few minutes if necessary.*

To fill the puffs, fit a clean pastry bag with a star tip. Fill the bag with the custard. Puncture the bottom of each pastry with the pastry tip and fill it with custard. Set aside.

To make the caramel glaze, have ready a shallow pan filled with ice water. Stir the sugar with 1/2 cup cold water in a 3- to 4-cup saucepan until the sugar is completely moistened. Do not stir again during the cooking process as this may cause the syrup to crystallize. Cover and bring to a simmer over medium heat. Uncover and wash down the sides of the pan with a wet pastry brush. Cover and cook for 2 minutes to dissolve the sugar completely. Uncover and cook until the syrup looks pale amber when 1 or 2 drops are spooned onto a white saucer. Swirl the pan gently and continue to cook until drops are medium amber. Plunge the bottom of the saucepan in the pan of ice water for a few seconds to stop the cooking. Prop the caramel pan in a tilted position.

Holding a pastry with your fingers or a pair of ice tongs, dip the top about halfway into the caramel (if using your fingers, be very careful) and set it right side up on a cookie sheet lined with wax paper or parchment. Repeat until all of the pastries are dipped. *Pastries may be prepared to this point and refrigerated up to several hours.* Set caramel aside in the saucepan until needed.

Five to 10 minutes before serving, heap the glazed pastries into a serving bowl or pile them on a platter. Following the instructions on page 111, heat the leftover caramel and spin the sugar. Serve as soon as possible.

Photograph on page 34

chocolate hazelnut roulade

SERVES 8 TO 10

This rustic-looking bûche de noël doesn't take three days and five different recipes! Add frills, such as meringue mushrooms, only if there's time. Substitute different nuts, or flavor the cream with brandy instead of coffee, or serve with raspberry or caramel sauce. No rules or limits here.

CAKE

1/4 cup hazelnuts, toasted and cooled, skins rubbed off

2 tablespoons all-purpose flour

6 ounces bittersweet or semisweet chocolate, coarsely chopped

8 tablespoons (1 stick) unsalted butter, cut into pieces

4 eggs, separated

3/4 cup sugar

1/8 teaspoon cream of tartar

2 to 3 tablespoons unsweetened Dutch-process cocoa powder

FILLING

1 cup heavy cream, cold

2 teaspoons instant espresso or coffee powder

1/2 teaspoon vanilla extract

11/2 to 2 tablespoons sugar

Powdered sugar, for dusting (optional)

EQUIPMENT

16 x 12- or 17x11-inch jelly-roll pan, lined with parchment paper, wax paper, or foil

CHOCOLATE NOTE

You can use any domestic bittersweet or semisweet chocolate that does not have a percentage on the label, or any boutique or imported brand marked 50 to 72 percent.

Preheat the oven to 350°F.

To make the roulade, in a clean, dry food processor bowl, combine the nuts with the flour and pulse until the nuts are finely ground. Set aside.

In the top of a double boiler over barely simmering water or in a heatproof bowl set into a skillet of barely simmering water, melt the chocolate and butter, stirring occasionally, until the mixture is melted and smooth. Remove from the heat. Or microwave on Medium (50 percent) power for about 2 minutes. Stir until smooth and completely melted. Set aside.

In a large bowl, whisk the egg yolks with 1/2 cup of the sugar until pale and thick. Stir in the warm chocolate mixture. Set aside.

In a clean, dry bowl, beat the egg whites and cream of tartar with an electric mixer on medium speed until soft peaks are formed. Gradually sprinkle in the remaining 1/4 cup of sugar, beating at high speed until stiff but not dry.

Using a rubber spatula, fold about one fourth of the egg whites and all of the hazelnut mixture into the chocolate mixture. Fold in the remaining whites. Turn the batter into the prepared pan and spread evenly. Bake until a toothpick inserted into the center of the cake comes out with moist crumbs, 12 to 15 minutes. Cool completely in the pan on a rack.

Sieve a light dusting of cocoa over a 16-inch sheet of foil, reserving the remaining cocoa. Invert the cooled cake on the foil and peel off the pan liner.

To make the filling, whip the cream with the espresso powder and vanilla until it begins to thicken. Sprinkle in the sugar and beat until the cream holds a soft shape. Spread the cream over the cake and, starting at a short edge, roll the cake using the foil to help you. At first the cake will crack as you roll it. Do not worry; the cracking will get less severe as the roulade gets fatter, and a little cracking on the finished roulade looks like tree bark, quite appetizing. Wrap the roulade in foil and refrigerate until serving.

To serve, unwrap the roulade and transfer it to a platter. Sieve a little more cocoa over it or use a little powdered sugar for contrast.

Photograph on page 35

bittersweet chocolate truffles

These are still my favorite chocolate truffles, but the original recipe, from *Cocolat,* included raw egg. Here the egg is adequately heated to prevent salmonella. The truffles are as good as ever. A dozen or so nestled into a gold foil bag tied with a pretty ribbon is a popular teacher gift at Christmas. My daughter gets excellent grades.

8 ounces bittersweet or semisweet chocolate, finely chopped

6 tablespoons (3/4 stick) unsalted butter, cut into small pieces

1 egg yolk, at room temperature

1/4 cup boiling water

1/3 cup unsweetened Dutch-process cocoa powder

EQUIPMENT   Instant-read thermometer

CHOCOLATE NOTE   You can use any domestic bittersweet or semisweet chocolate that does not have a percentage on the label, or any boutique or imported brand marked 50 to 62 percent. Or, substitute 6 ounces chocolate marked 64 to 66 percent, or substitute 5 1/3 ounces chocolate marked 70 percent and dissolve 2 teaspoons sugar in the hot water before adding it.

To make the truffles, place the chocolate and butter in a 4- to 6-cup heatproof bowl set in a wide skillet of barely simmering water over low heat. Stir frequently until the chocolate and butter are completely melted and smooth. Remove the bowl and set aside. Leave the skillet on low heat.

Place the egg yolk in a small bowl. Gradually whisk in the boiling water. Place the bowl in the skillet and stir constantly until the yolk mixture thickens slightly to the consistency of light cream and registers between 160° and 165°F. on an instant-read thermometer. Remove from the skillet and scrape the yolk mixture immediately over the melted chocolate.

Stir gently, without whisking or beating, just until the egg is completely incorporated and the mixture is smooth. Pour through a fine strainer into a clean bowl. Cover and chill until firm, 2 hours or more.

To form the truffles, remove the truffle mixture from the refrigerator and allow it to soften about 30 minutes if the mixture is very hard. Pour cocoa into a pie plate. Dip a melon baller or small spoon into a glass of hot water, wipe off the excess water, and scrape across the surface of the chilled truffle mixture to form a rough 1-inch ball. Pinch the truffle into shape with your fingers if necessary; it should not be perfectly round. Deposit the truffle into the cocoa. Repeat with the remaining truffle mixture. Gently shake the pie plate to coat truffles with cocoa. *Store truffles, tightly covered and refrigerated, up to 2 weeks or freeze up to 3 months.*

Bittersweet Mint Truffles: Add 1 teaspoon peppermint extract to the melted chocolate with the egg mixture.

very rich hot chocolate | This is decadently rich! Demitasse portions are advised. This recipe brings out the special flavor characteristics of any chocolate you use. Try it with any good semisweet or bittersweet chocolate.

3 ounces semisweet or bittersweet chocolate, chopped into small pieces

3/4 cup boiling water

3/4 cup milk

Whipped cream, for serving (optional)

Place the chocolate in a small saucepan. Pour a little of the boiling water over the chocolate and stir until the chocolate is melted. Add the rest of the boiling water and the milk. Heat the mixture, whisking constantly, until it is hot but not boiling. For the best flavor and texture, avoid exceeding 180°F. Serve immediately or set aside and reheat gently before serving.

chocolate cranberry babka

Babka or brioche? It might depend on which holiday you are celebrating when you serve this festive bread. The best babka dough is the same as for the luxurious butter and egg–enriched breakfast bread known as brioche. Here, with swirls of dark chocolate, cinnamon, and festive dried fruit, brioche becomes babka.

DOUGH

3 cups bread flour

20 tablespoons (2$^1/_2$ sticks) unsalted butter, cold

1 envelope (1 scant tablespoon) active dry yeast

1 teaspoon plus $^1/_3$ cup granulated sugar

$^1/_4$ cup warm water (105° to 115°F.)

5 eggs, cold

1$^1/_2$ teaspoons salt

FILLING

$^3/_4$ cup (packed) light brown sugar

$^2/_3$ cup semisweet chocolate chips

2 tablespoons unsweetened cocoa powder

2 tablespoons instant coffee or espresso powder

2 teaspoons ground cinnamon

1 cup dried cranberries or cherries

EQUIPMENT

8- to 10-cup tube pan, greased

To make the babka, spread the flour in a wide baking pan. Freeze at least 30 minutes or until needed.

Using the paddle attachment of a heavy-duty mixer, beat the cold butter only until creamy, smooth, and free of lumps when pinched between your fingers. Scrape the butter into a mound on wax paper and refrigerate. Proceed with the recipe right away; a long delay will reharden the butter.

Dissolve the yeast and 1 teaspoon of sugar in the warm water. Pour the dissolved yeast in the mixer bowl. Attach the dough hook. Add the remaining $^1/_3$ cup sugar, eggs, salt, and the flour and mix until blended. Knead the dough on medium speed for 5 minutes. After kneading period the dough will be very soft, sticky, and elastic. It will all be wrapped around the dough hook. Add the cold creamed butter in several pieces, pushing it into the dough, and beat with the hook until thoroughly incorporated. Stop several times to scrape the dough from the bowl and hook. Scrape the dough into a bowl, cover, and refrigerate overnight.

Mix the filling ingredients and cover.

Up to 24 hours later, scrape the cold dough out onto a floured surface. Use a rolling pin to roll the dough into a rectangle about 18 x 12 x $^1/_2$ inches. Scatter the filling evenly over the dough, leaving a 1-inch margin on 1 long edge. Moisten the margin with water. Beginning at the long edge opposite the margin, roll the dough up like a jelly roll. Press firmly to seal the roll. With the seam facing down, cut 18 slices, each about 1 inch thick. Toss the slices gently into the pan, without particularly arranging them. If you lay them flat in the pan, they will not stick together properly. Adjust the slices to reach the same level in the pan. Cover loosely with plastic wrap and let rise in a warm place until doubled, about 2 hours.

Preheat the oven to 350°F. Place the pan on a baking sheet. Bake until the top is deeply browned and the bottom of the pan sounds hollow when tapped or until an instant-read thermometer registers 200°F. when inserted in the center of the bread, 50 to 60 minutes. Cool in the pan on a rack.

black-and-white apricot pecan cake

Lighter and moister than a pound cake, this marbled loaf is fragrant with bourbon and studded with just enough tangy dried apricots and toasted pecans to make it irresistible with coffee or tea, and it's a great gift for the holidays. Double the recipe and keep one in the freezer for unexpected company.

1/2 cup diced (1/4 inch) moist dried apricot halves*

3 tablespoons bourbon

5 tablespoons buttermilk, at room temperature

1 teaspoon vanilla extract

2 1/2 tablespoons plus 1 cup sugar

2 1/2 tablespoons unsweetened Dutch-process cocoa powder

1/2 teaspoon instant coffee or espresso powder

1 1/4 cups all-purpose flour

1/4 teaspoon baking powder

1/4 teaspoon baking soda

1/4 teaspoon salt

8 tablespoons (1 stick) unsalted butter, at room temperature

2 eggs, at room temperature

1/2 cup pecan halves, toasted and cooled, coarsely chopped

EQUIPMENT   8-cup plain or fancy tube pan

I like the more intense flavor of dried apricot halves rather than the lighter-colored whole dried apricots.

To make the cake, in a small cup, combine the diced apricots with the bourbon and soak about 15 minutes. Add the buttermilk and vanilla. Set aside.

Position a rack in the lower third of the oven. Preheat the oven to 325°F. Spray the insides of the pan, including the tube, with vegetable oil spray.

In a small bowl, whisk 2 1/2 tablespoons of the sugar with the cocoa, coffee powder, and 2 1/2 tablespoons water until smooth. Set aside.

Sift the flour, baking powder, baking soda, and salt together 3 times. Set aside.

In a medium to large bowl, with an electric mixer (using the flat beater or paddle instead of the whisk on heavy-duty stand mixers), beat the butter for a few seconds until creamy. Add the remaining 1 cup of sugar in a steady stream and continue to beat at high speed with a hand-held mixer or medium speed with a heavy-duty stand mixer until light and fluffy, about 4 minutes. Meanwhile break the eggs into a cup and whisk them to combine the whites and yolks. Beat the eggs into the butter mixture gradually, beating constantly for about 2 minutes.

Stop the mixer and add one third of the flour mixture to the bowl. Beat on low speed only until no flour is visible. Stop the mixer and add half of the liquid and apricots. Beat only until the liquid is absorbed. Repeat with half of the remaining flour mixture, then all of the remaining liquid and apricots, and finally the remaining flour, stopping the mixer each time you add ingredients, then beating on low speed only enough to incorporate the ingredients. Stir in the pecans. Remove a scant cup of batter and fold it into the cocoa mixture.

Cover the bottom of the prepared pan with three quarters of the plain batter, in large irregular dollops. Cover with dollops of the chocolate batter. Spoon dollops of the remaining plain batter at intervals over the chocolate batter so that chocolate batter is still visible between dollops. Using a dinner knife, marble the batters in small overlapping circles gradually traveling around the center tube. I usually go around twice, trying to make the top of the batter look interesting but also trying not to blend the 2 batters together too much. Bake until a wooden skewer plunged into the center of the cake comes out clean, 50 to 55 minutes. Cool the cake in the pan on a rack for 10 minutes before unmolding.

Cool completely on a rack before wrapping and storing. *Cake keeps, well wrapped, for several days, or freeze up to 3 months.*

Variations: Substitute dark or golden raisins for apricots, or use diced dried pears, peaches, or prunes, fresh or dried cranberries, dried cherries—the list goes on. Pulverize the nuts with the flour in a food processor for a textural variation.

chocolate blini with berry caviar

Velvety indulgent chocolate pancakes for New Year's Eve, or brunch on New Year's Day, or any other day when chocolate for breakfast is required.

3/4 cup all-purpose flour

2 tablespoons granulated sugar

2 teaspoons baking powder

1/8 teaspoon salt

8 tablespoons (1 stick) unsalted butter

1/4 cup unsweetened cocoa powder, natural or Dutch process

1/2 cup milk

1/4 cup (packed) brown sugar

1/2 teaspoon instant coffee powder

1 egg

1/2 teaspoon vanilla extract

Butter, for the skillet

1 cup crème fraîche or lightly sweetened whipped cream

1 pint fresh raspberries, crushed lightly with a fork to resemble caviar

EQUIPMENT   A large skillet or griddle

To make the blini, in a medium bowl, mix the flour, granulated sugar, baking powder, and salt. Set aside.

Melt the butter in a small saucepan. Stir in the cocoa until smooth and hot. Gradually stir in the milk and heat to lukewarm. Off heat, whisk in the brown sugar, coffee powder, egg, and vanilla, stirring until the mixture is completely smooth. Pour the contents of the saucepan over the flour mixture and stir until the dry ingredients are completely moistened.

Heat the skillet over low heat until hot and coat the pan with butter. Pour 3-inch pancakes and cook on low heat until bubbles form around the edges. Flip the cakes and cook until lightly colored on the bottom and cooked through in the center. Serve immediately or keep hot in a 200°F. oven, loosely covered with foil, for up to 20 minutes. Serve with the crème fraîche and berries.

chocolate-laced holiday stollen

You might imagine stollen on a festive holiday breakfast table laden with silver and linens, perhaps with steaming Viennese coffee and a bowl of thick cream. As for me, I have fond memories of nibbling rich and rummy stollen while working the Christmas crack-of-dawn shift in my bakery, Cocolat, during the late 1970s.

1/3 cup diced candied lemon peel

1/3 cup dark raisins

1/3 cup golden raisins

1/3 cup dried cherries

1/3 cup dark rum

1 envelope (1 scant tablespoon) active dry yeast

1/2 teaspoon plus 1/3 cup granulated sugar

2 tablespoons warm water (105° to 115°F.)

1/2 cup milk

1 teaspoon salt

6 tablespoons (3/4 stick) butter, at room temperature

1/2 teaspoon almond extract

3 cups bleached all-purpose flour

1 egg, at room temperature

1 teaspoon grated orange zest

1 cup blanched almonds, toasted

1 cup chocolate chips

Flour, for dusting

1/4 cup powdered sugar

EQUIPMENT

Heavy-duty stand mixer with a dough hook

1 large baking sheet, lined with parchment paper or greased

1 large baking sheet, unlined

Instant-read thermometer

To make the stollen, combine the candied lemon peel, dried fruit, and rum in a resealable plastic bag. Let stand overnight, turning the bag over once or twice.

Set a colander over a bowl. Drain the fruit, reserving the rum.

In a small bowl, dissolve the yeast and 1/2 teaspoon of the sugar in the warm water. Set aside.

In a small saucepan, heat the milk to a simmer. Remove from the heat and add the salt and butter. Stir until the butter is melted. Stir in the almond extract and set aside until lukewarm.

In a mixer bowl, combine the flour, remaining sugar, milk mixture, egg, orange zest, dissolved yeast, and reserved rum. Using the dough hook, mix until combined, then knead the dough on low speed for 10 minutes. Scrape the dough onto a well-floured surface. Pat it into an oblong about 16 x 12 inches. Scatter the almonds and chocolate chips evenly over the dough. Roll the dough up, starting at one short end. Pat the dough out again, sprinkle it with the drained fruit, and roll it up. Shape the dough into a ball and place it in a large clean bowl. Dust the dough with flour and cover the bowl tightly with plastic wrap and let rise in a warm place until the dough is half again as large, about 2 hours.

Scrape the dough onto a well-floured surface. Pat out to form a 12x8-inch oval and fold it lengthwise. Press down firmly on the folded edge to seal it. Place the stollen on the lined pan. Cover loosely with plastic wrap and let rise until half again as large, about 1 1/2 hours.

Position a rack in the lower third of the oven. Preheat the oven to 350°F.

Place the baking sheet with the stollen on a second, unlined baking sheet to reduce browning on the bottom and remove the plastic wrap. Bake for 30 minutes. Tent the stollen loosely with foil, and bake 15 minutes more, or until the loaf sounds hollow when tapped on the bottom or an instant-read thermometer registers 200°F. when inserted in the center of the thickest part of the loaf. Carefully (to avoid breaking the loaf) transfer the stollen to a large rack to cool completely. Wrap airtight to store.

Before serving, dust generously with powdered sugar.

breakfast valentines

For a special Valentine's breakfast or for tea, the quintessential chocolate scone to nibble with barely sweetened whipped cream or crème fraîche and jam.

1½ cups all-purpose flour

²/₃ cup sugar

1 tablespoon baking powder if using Dutch-process cocoa, or a scant 1 teaspoon baking soda if using natural cocoa

¼ teaspoon salt

10 tablespoons (1¼ sticks) melted unsalted butter, hot

¼ cup plus 2 tablespoons unsweetened cocoa powder, Dutch process or natural

1 egg, cold

¼ cup plus 2 tablespoons cold milk

Barely sweetened whipped cream, for serving (optional)

Crème fraîche, for serving (optional)

Jam, for serving (optional)

Berries, for serving (optional)

EQUIPMENT

A 2½-inch heart-shaped biscuit or cookie cutter

1 baking sheet, preferably lined with parchment, otherwise ungreased

Position a rack in the center of the oven. Preheat the oven to 400°F.

To make the valentines, in a medium bowl, mix the flour, sugar, baking powder or soda, and salt.

In a separate bowl, mix the hot butter and cocoa until smooth. Stir in the egg and milk. Pour the wet mixture over the dry ingredients. Fold gently with a rubber spatula, scraping the ingredients from the sides of the bowl to the center, just until all of the flour mixture is moistened. Do not try to make a smooth dough.

Place the dough on a sheet of wax paper and pat it into a 10 x 5-inch rectangle (assuming your heart-shaped cutter is 2½ inches). Chill the dough for about 15 minutes to firm it up slightly.

Cut out 8 hearts. Use dough scraps to form 2 more hearts. Transfer the hearts to the baking sheet. Bake until the tops are dry and cracked and the bottoms have begun to color, about 12 minutes. Serve warm or at room temperature. Serve plain, dusted with powdered sugar, or with barely sweetened whipped cream or crème fraîche with jam or fresh berries, if desired.

hot chocolate soufflés

Forget light and ethereal. I like a chocolate soufflé that is dark, rich, and substantial. Forget fussy last-minute preparation. For a Valentine's or intimate dinner before the fireplace, I like a simple, indestructible soufflé that can be prepared in advance.

About 2 tablespoons unsalted butter, softened, to butter the soufflé cups

About 2 tablespoons granulated sugar, to coat the soufflé cups

8 ounces bittersweet or semisweet chocolate, coarsely chopped

1 tablespoon unsalted butter

1 tablespoon all-purpose flour

1/3 cup milk

3 egg yolks

2 teaspoons vanilla extract

4 egg whites

1/8 teaspoon cream of tartar

1/3 cup granulated sugar

2 to 3 tablespoons powdered sugar, for dusting (optional)

Lightly sweetened whipped cream

EQUIPMENT

Eight 6-ounce soufflé cups

1 cookie sheet, unlined

Preheat the oven to 375°F.

Butter the bottom and sides of the soufflé cups. To coat with sugar, fill one of them with the granulated sugar. Tilt the cup and rotate it over a second cup, until the sides are completely coated with sugar. Pour excess sugar into the second cup and repeat until all the cups are coated with sugar. Discard excess sugar.

To make the soufflés, melt the chocolate in a medium to large bowl set in a pan of barely simmering water, stirring occasionally, until melted and smooth. Remove from heat. Or melt in a microwave on Medium (50 percent) for about 3 minutes and 30 seconds. Stir until smooth. Set aside.

In a small saucepan, melt the butter. Add the flour and cook, stirring constantly, for 1 or 2 minutes. On medium heat, add the milk gradually, whisking briskly until the mixture forms a smooth sauce. Continue cooking and whisking for 1 to 2 minutes, or until the sauce thickens. Off heat, whisk in the egg yolks and 1 teaspoon of the vanilla. Scrape the sauce over the chocolate and whisk until blended. Set aside.

In a clean, dry large bowl, beat the egg whites with the cream of tartar at medium speed until soft peaks form when the beaters are lifted. Gradually sprinkle in the granulated sugar and continue to beat on high speed until the egg whites are stiff but not dry. Fold one quarter of the whites into the chocolate mixture to lighten it, then fold in the remaining whites. Divide the mixture evenly among the sugared cups, filling them up to three quarters full. *Soufflés may be prepared to this point, covered, and refrigerated up to 3 days before serving.*

Bake the soufflés on a cookie sheet until a wooden skewer plunged into the center tests moist but not completely gooey or runny, 15 to 17 minutes. Soufflés will puff and crack before they are done.

Remove the soufflés from the oven and lightly sift powdered sugar over them, if desired. Serve immediately with the whipped cream.

irish coffee chocolate mousse

Irish whiskey notwithstanding, this looks and tastes like a classic French chocolate mousse, with its rich smooth flavor and dense but foamy texture. Because eggs are the secret to great chocolate mousse (in my opinion), I've designed this recipe to avoid the risks associated with raw eggs.

4 ounces bittersweet or semisweet chocolate, chopped into small pieces

1 cup heavy cream

1 1/2 teaspoons instant espresso powder

3 to 4 teaspoons Irish whiskey

2 eggs

2 tablespoons plus 4 teaspoons sugar

1/2 teaspoon vanilla extract

EQUIPMENT

Instant-read thermometer

6 to 8 ramekins or dessert cups

CHOCOLATE NOTE

You can use any domestic semisweet or bittersweet chocolate that does not have a percentage on the label, or any boutique or imported brand marked 50 to 62 percent.

To make the mousse, place the chocolate, 1/3 cup of cream, and 1/4 teaspoon of the espresso powder in a heatproof bowl. Set the bowl in a skillet of barely simmering water. Stir frequently until the chocolate is completely melted and smooth. Remove the bowl from the skillet, stir in the whiskey, and set aside.

In a heatproof medium bowl, whisk the eggs with 1 tablespoon water and 2 tablespoons of the sugar until well blended. Set the bowl in the skillet and whisk the eggs constantly (to prevent them from scrambling) over not-even-simmering water until they register 160°F. on an instant-read thermometer. Remove the bowl from the skillet and beat at high speed with an electric mixer until the eggs have a texture like softly whipped cream, 3 to 4 minutes. Fold one quarter of the eggs into the chocolate. Scrape the chocolate mixture over the remaining whipped eggs and continue to fold just until evenly incorporated. Divide the mousse among the ramekins. Chill at least 1 hour, or until set, before serving.

In a chilled bowl with chilled beaters, beat the remaining 2/3 cup of cream with the vanilla, the remaining 4 teaspoons sugar, and the remaining 1 1/4 teaspoons espresso powder until nearly stiff. Top each mousse with a dollop of cream before serving.

the ultimate flourless chocolate cake

I originally created this recipe for *Cook's Illustrated* magazine. It has the texture of a dense bittersweet chocolate mousse. Make it when you want an extreme chocolate indulgence—or need something to give up for Lent! Serve very thin slices with raspberry purée and whipped cream. Make the cake at least one day before serving.

8 eggs, cold

1 pound bittersweet or semisweet chocolate, coarsely chopped

16 tablespoons (2 sticks) unsalted butter, cut into 1/2-inch chunks

1/4 cup strong coffee or liqueur (optional)

SAUCE AND TOPPING

1 package (10 to 12 ounces) frozen raspberries, thawed, or 8 to 10 ounces fresh raspberries

Granulated sugar to taste

Powdered sugar, for decoration (optional)

1 cup heavy cream

1 teaspoon vanilla extract

EQUIPMENT

8-inch springform pan

Instant-read thermometer

CHOCOLATE NOTE

You can use any domestic semisweet or bittersweet chocolate that does not have a percentage on the label, or any boutique or imported brand marked 50 to 70 percent.

Position a rack in the lower third of the oven. Preheat the oven to 325°F.

To make the cake, line the bottom of the springform pan with parchment paper and grease the sides. Set the pan on a wide sheet of heavy-duty foil and wrap the foil up the sides without tearing it. Set the pan in a larger baking pan or a roasting pan. Bring a kettle of water to a boil.

Preferably using a hand-held mixer, beat the eggs at high speed until the volume of the eggs doubles to about 1 quart, 5 minutes. If you have to use a heavy-duty mixer, use the whisk attachment and speed 6 and beat to the same volume, which will take about the same amount of time. Melt the chocolate and butter, with coffee or liqueur, if using, in a large heatproof bowl either set in a pan of barely simmering water or in the microwave on Medium (50 percent) power, stirring frequently for 4 to 6 minutes or until the mixture is smooth and warm (about 115°F.).

Fold one third of the egg foam into the chocolate mixture with a large rubber spatula until just a few streaks of egg are still visible. Fold in half of the remaining foam in the same way. Fold the remaining foam into the batter until completely incorporated.

Scrape the batter into the prepared springform and smooth the surface. Set the roasting pan on the oven rack and pour enough boiling water into the pan to come about halfway up the side of the springform. Bake until the cake has risen slightly, the edges are just beginning to set, a thin glazed crust (like a brownie) has formed on the surface, and an instant-read thermometer inserted halfway into the center of the cake registers 140°F., 20 to 25 minutes. Remove the springform from the water bath and set on a wire rack. Cool to room temperature. Cover and refrigerate overnight to mellow. *Cake can be kept covered and refrigerated up to 4 days.*

To make the sauce, if using frozen raspberries, drain them and reserve the juice. Place fresh or drained frozen berries in the bowl of a food processor. Pulse briefly but not until perfectly smooth. Press the purée through a strainer to remove the seeds. Add some of the reserved juice, if desired. If the purée seems too tart, sweeten it to taste. Cover and refrigerate until serving.

About 30 minutes before serving, remove the springform pan sides, invert the cake onto a sheet of wax paper, peel off the parchment liner, and turn the cake right side up on a serving platter.

To serve, sieve the cake lightly with powdered sugar, if desired. Whip the cream with the vanilla and 2 teaspoons of sugar or more to taste until nearly stiff. Serve slim slices on a pool of raspberry sauce with a dollop of whipped cream on top.

chocolate mardi gras fondue

I have never seen anyone dip anything (even a finger) into chocolate without a smile. Although this festive, simple party dessert is a year-round opportunity to use the season's best and ripest fruit, I am partial to the time between darkest winter and early spring, when citrus fruit and bananas and dried fruits cry out for chocolate.

10 ounces bittersweet or semisweet chocolate, chopped into small pieces

1/2 to 3/4 cup milk, half-and-half, or heavy cream, or 1/2 to 3/4 cup milk plus 2 tablespoons unsalted butter

1/2 teaspoon vanilla extract

IDEAS FOR DIPPING Kumquats or segments of seedless clementines, oranges, or ruby grapefruit

Chunks of pineapple

Chunks of fresh coconut or large curls of dried coconut

Chunks of banana

Dried fruit such as apricot, mango, papaya, pineapple, or Bing cherries

Strips of good-quality candied orange, grapefruit, or lemon peel

Cubes of pound cake or angel food cake, or toasted cubes of brioche or challah

Cigarette cookies, fan wafers, graham crackers or digestive biscuits, or pretzels

Marshmallows or meringues

Toasted shaved almonds (to sprinkle on *after* dipping)

Tip: If possible, separate the citrus into segments without breaking the membrane. If you set the segments on a rack to dry in a warm place or in the oven, preheated to 200°F., then turned off for several hours, the membrane will dry like crisp paper and the juices will burst in your mouth when you take a bite.

To make the sauce, in a small bowl, combine the chocolate and 1/2 cup milk or cream and melt gently in a barely simmering water bath or microwave on Medium (50 percent) power for about 2 minutes. Stir until smooth. Add more liquid if the sauce seems too thick or looks curdled. Remove from the heat and stir in the vanilla. Use warm fondue immediately or set aside until needed and rewarm briefly.

Choose a selection of fruit and other dippables, with an eye to variety of color, flavor, and texture. And don't forget to include some children's favorites as well. Arrange on a platter or in pretty bowls.

Have forks, skewers, or pretty (or goofy) swizzle sticks available for guests to dip with. If the fondue gets too thick or cool, reheat gently (without boiling) for 1 minute in the microwave on Medium (50 percent) power or set in a pan of barely simmering water. Leftover sauce keeps several days in the refrigerator. It is a perfect topping for ice cream.

Note: This is a versatile recipe that can be tailored to your taste and the type of chocolate you are using. For the most intense chocolate fondue, use milk, rather than half-and-half or cream, and omit the butter. For even greater intensity, choose a bittersweet chocolate labeled anywhere from 66 to 70 percent and use the greater amount of liquid called for. Butter or cream results in a softer, mellower chocolate flavor.

spring

Chocolate lends an exuberant, playful spirit to all the rites and rituals of spring. A chocolate fancier's imagination comes alive, and taste buds are ready for something new—bright tangy strawberries, zesty lemons, creamy cheeses, even salted pretzels. When at Passover I can't decide between a rich, intensely bittersweet torte or one that's moist and light with subtle sophistication, I simply make them both. Chocolate can be charming. Twiggy chocolate baskets overflow with chocolate-drenched strawberries, chocolate truffles, fanciful fungi, or jelly beans. Eggs of every ilk appear at Easter, from Giant Krispy Eggs to elegant marbled cream-puff eggs filled with ice cream. Sensational cheesecakes are de rigueur, with swirls of mocha or lemony white chocolate. Spring chocolate is truly celebratory.

chocolate hamantaschen

Look elsewhere for traditional poppy seeds, prunes, or apricots. Here, Haman's hat brims with bittersweet brownie filling. Please don't save these for a Jewish holiday... great chocolate and vanilla cookies should be shared anytime.

FILLING

- 8 tablespoons (1 stick) unsalted butter
- 4 ounces unsweetened chocolate, coarsely chopped
- 3/4 cup sugar
- 1 teaspoon vanilla extract
- 1/4 teaspoon salt
- 2 eggs, cold
- 2 tablespoons all-purpose flour

COOKIE DOUGH

- 2 cups all-purpose flour
- 1/2 teaspoon baking powder
- 1/4 teaspoon salt
- 8 tablespoons (1 stick) unsalted butter, softened but not squishy
- 1 cup sugar
- 1 egg
- 1 1/2 teaspoons vanilla extract

EQUIPMENT

- Cookie sheets, lined with parchment paper
- 3-inch round cookie cutter

To make the filling, melt the butter with the chocolate in the top of a double boiler. Stir frequently until the mixture is melted and smooth, then remove the top of the double boiler from the heat. Stir in the sugar, vanilla, and salt. Add the eggs, one at a time, stirring in the first until incorporated before adding the second. Stir in the flour and beat with a spoon until the mixture is smooth and glossy and comes away from the sides of the pan, about 1 minute. Scrape into a small bowl, cover, and refrigerate until needed.

To make the cookie dough, mix the flour, baking powder, and salt together thoroughly with a whisk or a fork. Set aside.

In a large bowl, beat the butter and sugar with an electric mixer until light and fluffy, 3 to 4 minutes. Beat in the egg and vanilla. On low speed, beat in the flour mixture just until incorporated. Form the dough into 2 flat patties. Wrap and refrigerate the patties at least until firm enough to roll, preferably several hours or overnight.

Position racks in the upper and lower thirds of the oven. Preheat the oven to 350°F.

Remove one of the patties from the refrigerator and let it sit until supple enough to roll but still quite firm. It will continue to soften as you work. Roll the dough between 2 pieces of wax paper or between heavy plastic sheets from a plastic bag to a thickness of

$1/8$ inch. Turn the dough over once or twice while rolling it out to check for deep wrinkles; if it's necessary, peel off and smooth the paper over the dough before continuing to roll it. When the dough is thin enough, peel off the top sheet of paper or plastic and keep it in front of you. Invert the dough onto that sheet. Cut cookies as close together as possible, dipping the edges of the cutter in flour as necessary to prevent sticking. Press dough scraps together and set aside to reroll with scraps from the second patty.

Place cookies $1/2$ inch apart on the prepared cookie sheets. Scoop and place 1 level teaspoonful of filling in the center of each cookie. Bring 3 sides of each cookie up to partially cover the filling. Pinch the edges of each cookie to seal the corners. Bake until pale golden at the edges, rotating the cookie sheets from top to bottom and front to back halfway through the baking, about 12 minutes. Repeat until all the cookies are baked. Slide the parchment liners onto cooling racks. Cool the cookies completely before stacking or storing. *Although best on the day they are made, cookies keep 3 or 4 days in an airtight container.*

passover brownies

These brownies, baked at a high temperature then cooled quickly in ice water, are crusty on the outside but smooth and creamy within.

8 tablespoons (1 stick) unsalted butter or unsalted stick margarine

4 ounces unsweetened chocolate, coarsely chopped

1¼ cups sugar

1 teaspoon vanilla extract

¼ teaspoon salt

2 eggs

⅓ cup matzo cake meal

⅔ cup walnut or pecan pieces (optional)

EQUIPMENT

8-inch square pan (not glass), lined across the bottom and up 2 sides with parchment paper or foil

Position a rack in the lower third of the oven. Preheat the oven to 400°F.

Melt the butter with the chocolate in the top of a double boiler or in a medium heatproof bowl set in a pan of barely simmering water. Stir frequently until the mixture is melted and smooth. Remove the top of the double boiler from the heat; stir in the sugar, vanilla, and salt. Add the eggs, one at a time, stirring until incorporated before adding the next. Stir in the cake meal and beat with a wooden spoon until the batter is smooth and glossy and comes away from the sides of the pan, about 1 minute. Stir in the nuts, if using. Scrape the batter into the pan and spread evenly.

Bake until the batter just begins to pull away from the edges of the pan, 20 minutes. The surface of the brownies will look dry but a toothpick inserted in the center will still be quite gooey.

While the brownies are baking, clear space in the freezer or prepare an ice bath instead: Fill a roasting pan or large baking pan with ice cubes and water about ¾ inch deep. When the brownies are ready, remove the pan from the oven and set it immediately in the freezer or ice bath, taking care not to splash water on the brownies. When they're cool, slide a knife between the pan and the brownies on the unlined sides. Lift the ends of the parchment or foil liner and transfer the brownies to a cutting board. Cut into 16 squares. *Store in an airtight container for 2 to 3 days.*

passover chocolate nut sponge torte

Traditional Passover cakes used to fall into one of two camps: the light but horribly dry or the moist but leaden. This sophisticated almond cake blessedly defies tradition; it is light and moist, gently chocolatey, and very flavorful.

1 cup whole blanched almonds

2 tablespoons matzo cake meal

2 tablespoons potato starch

1 tablespoon instant coffee powder

6 ounces bittersweet or semisweet chocolate, coarsely chopped

Grated zest of 1 medium orange

9 eggs, separated, at room temperature

1 cup sugar

Lightly sweetened whipped cream (optional)

EQUIPMENT 9- or 10-inch flat-bottomed tube pan, preferably with a removable bottom, ungreased

Preheat the oven to 350°F. If the pan does not have a removable bottom, line the bottom with parchment paper or grease the bottom and coat it with matzo meal or flour.

In a food processor, combine the almonds, cake meal, potato starch, coffee powder, chocolate, and orange zest. Pulse until most of the almonds are finely ground (it's OK if some are a little coarser). Set aside.

In a large bowl, beat the egg yolks with 1/2 cup of the sugar until very thick and pale yellow. Set aside. Wash and dry the beaters.

In another large bowl, with clean, dry beaters, beat the egg whites until they are foamy. Gradually add the remaining 1/2 cup of sugar and beat until the egg whites are nearly stiff. Using a rubber spatula, fold one quarter of the egg whites into the yolk mixture. Scrape half of the remaining egg whites and half of the nut mixture over the yolk mixture and fold together. Repeat with the remaining egg whites and nut mixture. Spoon the batter gently into the pan and smooth the surface. Bake until the cake springs back when lightly pressed and a wooden skewer inserted into the center comes out free of batter but possibly coated with melted chocolate, 45 to 50 minutes. Cool the cake in the pan, right side up, on a wire rack.

To unmold, press a slim knife or small metal spatula flat around the insides of the pan to detach the cake without tearing it. Detach the cake from the tube the same way, using a skewer instead of a knife. Remove the sides of the pan or invert the pan to remove the cake, then peel off the paper liner and transfer the cake to a serving platter. Serve plain or with lightly sweetened whipped cream, if desired.

passover gâteau au chocolat | Why is this cake different from all other Passover cakes? It has a rich and intensely chocolate flavor with a texture as light and creamy as a mousse. Fresh raspberries, with or without whipped cream, are magical accompaniments. For best flavor, make the cake one day before serving.

1/4 cup whole almonds, blanched or unblanched

3 tablespoons matzo cake meal

9 ounces bittersweet or semisweet chocolate, coarsely chopped

16 tablespoons (2 sticks) unsalted butter or unsalted stick margarine, cut into pieces

6 eggs, separated

Grated zest of 1 medium orange

1/3 cup (packed) light brown sugar

2/3 cup granulated sugar

1/8 teaspoon salt

Cocoa powder or powdered sugar, for dusting (optional)

EQUIPMENT   9-inch springform pan, 2 1/2 to 3 inches deep, ungreased

CHOCOLATE NOTE   You can use any domestic semisweet or bittersweet chocolate that does not have a percentage on the label, or any boutique or imported brand marked 50 to 72 percent.

Preheat the oven to 375°F.

In a food processor, pulse the almonds and cake meal until the almonds are very finely ground. Set aside.

Melt the chocolate and butter in the top of a double boiler or in a small bowl placed in a skillet of barely simmering water, stirring occasionally until melted and smooth. Remove from the heat. Or microwave on

Medium (50 percent) power for 2 1/2 to 3 minutes. Stir until smooth and completely melted.

In a large bowl, whisk the egg yolks and orange zest with the brown sugar, 1/3 cup of the granulated sugar, and salt until pale and thick. Stir in the warm chocolate mixture. Set aside.

In a clean, dry mixing bowl, beat the egg whites at medium speed until they are foamy. Gradually sprinkle in the remaining 1/3 cup granulated sugar, beating at high speed until almost stiff. Fold about one quarter of the egg whites and all of the almond mixture into the yolk mixture. Fold in the remaining whites. Scrape the batter into the prepared pan and bake until a toothpick or wooden skewer plunged into the cake about 1 1/2 inches from the edge of the cake comes out clean, 30 to 35 minutes. The center of the cake will jiggle slightly when the pan is jostled and will still be gooey if tested. Set the cake on a rack to cool. The surface will crack and fall as it cools. *May be prepared to this point and will keep, covered, at room temperature, 2 to 3 days, or frozen up to 3 months. Bring to room temperature before serving.*

Slide a slim knife around the sides of the cake to release it. Remove the pan sides and transfer the cake, right side up, to a serving platter. Sprinkle a little cocoa (or powdered sugar if not for Passover) over the top before serving, if desired.

mocha marble cheesecake | I like cheesecakes with marbled
fillings because they are beautiful and self-decorating and because
I like to play with the juxtaposition of flavors. This one looks like
a marbled Easter egg.

CRUST

1 1/2 cups chocolate wafer crumbs

6 tablespoons (3/4 stick) melted butter

1/4 cup sugar

1 1/2 teaspoons instant espresso powder

FILLING

1 1/2 ounces milk chocolate, very finely chopped

3/4 teaspoon instant espresso or coffee powder

1 1/2 tablespoons boiling water

1 1/2 pounds cream cheese, at room temperature

1/2 cup sugar

1 1/2 teaspoons vanilla extract

2 eggs, at room temperature

EQUIPMENT

8-inch springform pan, greased

Position a rack in the lower third of the oven. Preheat the oven to 350°F.

To make the crust, in a medium bowl, use a fork to mix the chocolate wafer crumbs, melted butter, sugar, and instant espresso powder. Press the mixture evenly over the bottom and about halfway up the sides of the pan. Bake 10 minutes. Cool on a rack before filling. Grease the sides of the pan again, above the crust level, to prevent the filling from sticking to the pan in case it is deeper than the crust.

Lower the oven temperature to 325°F.

To make the filling, place the milk chocolate in a small bowl with the espresso powder. Pour the boiling water over and stir until smooth. Set aside.

In a medium mixing bowl, beat the cream cheese just until smooth, about 30 seconds. Scrape the bowl and beaters. Add the sugar and the vanilla and beat just until smooth and creamy, 1 to 2 minutes. Add 1 egg and beat just until incorporated. Scrape the bowl and beaters. Beat in the second egg. Stir 1 cup of the batter into the bowl of melted chocolate. Pour the remaining plain batter into the prepared crust and smooth the top. Pour or spoon pools or ribbons of milk chocolate batter over the plain batter, making sure to leave some plain batter showing. Jiggle the pan gently to level the batters. Marble the batters with a small spoon by gently stirring in small loopy circles until the colors are intermingled but not blended. Place the pan on a baking sheet.

Bake until the edges of the cake are puffed but the center looks moist and jiggles when tapped, 35 to 45 minutes. Remove the cake from the oven. If the batter is touching the sides of the pan above the height of the crust, slide a thin paring knife carefully around the edges of the pan to detach the cake, but do not remove the pan sides. Place the pan on a rack and cover the pan and the rack with a large inverted bowl or pot so that the cake cools slowly. Cover and refrigerate the cooled cake at least 5 hours, preferably 24 hours, before serving.

chocolate easter baskets

Chocolate-coated pretzel "twigs" lend themselves to elegant centerpieces filled with chocolate truffles or meringue mushrooms. Or, make a little nest for a child and fill it with jelly beans and foil-wrapped chocolate eggs. Let kids play with the sticky chocolate-coated pretzels on wax paper...and voilà: miniature log cabins, stick figures, and edible skyscrapers.

3 ounces semisweet or bittersweet chocolate

3 or more cups thin pretzel sticks, salted or unsalted

FILLING

Coffee Meringue Mushrooms (page 71)

Bittersweet Chocolate Truffles (page 38)

Candy, such as jelly beans, foil-wrapped chocolate eggs, etc.

EQUIPMENT

2-quart bowl or box, lined with plastic wrap, for a large basket or nest

Sheets of wax paper for small nests

Melt the chocolate in the top of a double boiler over barely simmering water or in the microwave on Medium (50 percent) power. Cool to lukewarm. In a medium bowl, pour most of the chocolate over the pretzels. Use a rubber spatula to turn the pretzels gently in the chocolate until they are lightly coated, adding as much of the rest of the chocolate as necessary. It's OK if some of the pretzel shows through the chocolate.

For a large basket or nest, scrape the pretzels into the lined bowl or box. Arrange the sticky pretzels against the sides of the container to resemble a basket or a nest. Shape small nests or wreaths on sheets of wax paper.

Refrigerate to set the chocolate. To unmold the large basket, lift the plastic liner from the container and peel it away from the pretzels. Fill with meringue mushrooms, chocolate truffles, or candy.

Photograph on page 72

coffee meringue mushrooms

These meringue mushrooms are crisp and delicious as well as decorative. Dark chocolate and coffee offset the sweetness of the meringue, but feel free to omit the coffee.

3 egg whites, at room temperature

¹/₈ teaspoon cream of tartar

³/₄ cup sugar, preferably superfine

1¹/₂ teaspoons instant coffee or espresso powder (optional)

About 2 teaspoons unsweetened cocoa powder, for dusting

2 ounces bittersweet or semisweet chocolate, cut into small pieces

EQUIPMENT

Baking sheet, lined with parchment paper

Large pastry bag

Plain pastry tip with a ¹/₂-inch opening

Position a rack in the center of the oven. Preheat the oven to 200°F.

In a clean, dry mixing bowl, beat the egg whites and cream of tartar on medium speed until soft peaks form when the beaters are lifted. On high speed, gradually add half of the sugar with all of the coffee powder, if using, about 1 tablespoon at a time. The mixture should stand in stiff glossy peaks when the beaters are lifted. Using a rubber spatula, fold in the remaining sugar. Scrape the meringue into the pastry bag. Pipe tall pointed "kisses" about 1 inch high to make mushroom stems. Do not worry if the tips bend over or sag. Pipe domes to make mushroom caps. Sieve a light dusting of cocoa over caps and stems and fan them or blow on them vigorously to blur the cocoa and give the mushrooms an authentic look. Bake until crisp and completely dry, 2 hours.

To assemble the mushrooms, place the chocolate in a small bowl set in a skillet of barely simmering water. Immediately turn off the heat and stir the chocolate until melted and smooth. Use a sharp knife to cut ¹/₄ to ¹/₂ inch off the tip of each stem, to create a flat surface. Spread a generous coating of melted chocolate over the flat side of several mushroom caps. Allow the chocolate to set partially before attaching the cut surface of the stems. Repeat until all of the mushrooms are assembled. Set assembled mushrooms aside until the chocolate has hardened and caps and stems are glued together. *Meringue mushrooms may be made 3 to 4 weeks in advance and stored at room temperature in an airtight container.*

Photograph on page 72

ice cream easter eggs

Egg-shaped cream puffs, filled with ice cream, are a splendid Easter version of profiteroles. They are pretty and delicious. Eat them quickly, before they melt.

4 tablespoons (1/2 stick) unsalted butter, cut into 8 pieces

2 teaspoons sugar

1/8 teaspoon salt

3 tablespoons milk

1/3 cup water

1/2 cup all-purpose flour, sifted after measuring

3 eggs, lightly whisked

FILLING AND GLAZE

Fast Fudge Frosting (page 105) and/or White Chocolate Glaze (page 82)

1 ounce white chocolate (if glazing with fast fudge) or semisweet chocolate (if glazing with white chocolate), finely chopped, for marbling

1 quart vanilla ice cream or chocolate, coffee, or coconut ice cream

EQUIPMENT

Heavy cookie sheet or sheets, greased and floured

Pastry bag

Plain pastry tip with a 5/8-inch opening (Ateco #808 or #809)

Tiny artist's brush or toothpick for marbling the glaze

Position a rack in the lower third of the oven. Preheat the oven to 400°F.

To make puffs, combine the butter, sugar, and salt with the milk and water in a 11/2- to 2-quart heavy-bottomed saucepan. Bring to a boil over medium heat, stirring occasionally, so that the butter is completely melted by the time the mixture boils. Remove the pot from the stove. Pour the flour all at once into the pot and stir with a wooden spoon to form a thick paste. Return the pot to medium heat and dry the paste slightly by stirring and pushing it all over the sides and bottom of the pot until the pot looks clean but coated with a buttery film.

Transfer the hot paste into the bowl of an electric mixer or a bowl in which you can operate a hand-held electric mixer. Mix for 1 minute to cool slightly. Pour about 2 tablespoons of the egg into the paste and mix until incorporated. Gradually, in 3 or 4 additions, add nearly all of the rest of the egg, beating well after each addition until the egg is absorbed and the paste is smooth, very thick, and shiny and falls slowly from a wooden spoon. Add the remaining egg judiciously, only if the paste seems too thick.

Fit the pastry bag with the plain tip and fill it with warm paste. Pipe egg-shape mounds about 2¼ inches long by 1¾ inches wide, about 2 inches apart, on the baking sheets or scoop a scant 3 tablespoons of batter in an oval shape. Brush gently with water. Place a pan of hot tap water on the floor of the oven.

Bake 1 sheet at a time until the pastries are puffed and golden brown, 20 to 25 minutes. Turn the oven temperature down to 375°F. Remove the pan of water. Cut into the side of each pastry with a sharp knife to release steam. Bake 5 to 10 minutes more, or until the pastries are deep golden brown and very firm and crisp to the touch. Turn the oven off and leave the pastries inside 5 minutes more. Remove and cool puffs on a rack. *Cooled pastries may be stored in an airtight container in the refrigerator up to 3 days, or frozen up to 1 month. Recrisp in a 400°F. oven for a few minutes, if necessary.*

Glaze the tops up to several hours before serving. Prepare the glaze and melt the chocolate for marbling. Use a serrated knife to cut the pastries in half horizontally. Remove any uncooked dough from the insides. Dip the top half of each in glaze, letting the excess drip back in the bowl. Turn the tops, glaze side up, and drizzle with streaks of melted chocolate. Drag a brush or toothpick back and forth through the glaze to make a pretty pattern. Repeat until all of the tops are glazed and marbled. Set tops aside at room temperature until serving. Scoop egg-shape scoops of ice cream and return them to the freezer in a wax paper–lined pan.

To serve, reheat the leftover glaze to the consistency of sauce. Place a scoop of ice cream on the bottom half of each pastry and top with the glazed half. Serve immediately. Pass the sauce separately.

Photograph on page 73

giant krispy egg | This beats the popular chocolate crunch bars by a long shot, and it's too delicious just for kids. Wrap it in colored foil or cellophane or nestle it in Easter grass and call it a prehistoric dinosaur egg.

1¼ pounds milk chocolate or semisweet, bittersweet, or white chocolate

3½ to 4 cups Rice Krispies

EQUIPMENT   Two-part plastic egg mold 5¾ inches long by 4¼ inches wide or smaller

Colored foil or cellophane and ribbon (optional)

Following the instructions on page 112, melt and temper the chocolate. Or simply melt 1 pound of chocolate without tempering it. Pour 3½ cups of the Rice Krispies over the chocolate and fold gently with a rubber spatula just until all of the Rice Krispies are coated. Add the remaining Rice Krispies if there appears to be enough chocolate to coat them. Turn the mixture into each half of the mold and level the surface. Spread the leftover mixture on wax paper and cool at room temperature. Refrigerate the egg for 30 minutes before unmolding.

If you have tempered the chocolate, keep the egg at room temperature, otherwise keep it refrigerated. Glue the 2 flat surfaces together with a little melted chocolate, if desired, to form a single large egg. Wrap in colored foil or cellophane tied with a ribbon, if desired.

chocolate-dipped strawberries | All you need for these is good
chocolate and fresh ripe strawberries. The key to keeping the chocolate
from turning dull and gray is chilling and drying the berries before
dipping, then refrigerating them immediately until ready to serve.
Always dip strawberries on the same day they will be served.

2 pints strawberries of mixed size or up to 3 dozen
large stemmed berries

8 ounces chocolate (bittersweet, semisweet, milk, or
white), coarsely chopped, not chocolate chips or
morsels

EQUIPMENT   2 cookie sheets, lined with wax or parchment paper
Fluted paper cups (optional)

Rinse the berries gently and spread to dry on a tray
lined with paper towels. Refrigerate. The berries
should be cold and as dry as possible before dipping.
If it's necessary, use a cupped hand to cradle each
berry gently in a soft dish towel or paper towel to
dry it completely.

Melt bittersweet or semisweet chocolate in the top of
a double boiler, or in a heatproof bowl set in a skillet
of barely simmering water, or in a microwave on
Medium (50 percent) power. Stir frequently until the
chocolate is melted and smooth. To melt white or
milk chocolate in a double boiler or water bath, bring
the water to a simmer, and then remove from heat
and wait 60 seconds before setting the container of
chocolate in it. Stir almost constantly. To melt in
the microwave, use Low (30 percent) power and stir

frequently. Chocolate should be warm and fluid, not
hot. Transfer the chocolate to a clean, dry 1-cup
glass measure or another container of similar shape.

Grasp a berry by the stem or the shoulders and dip
it about two thirds of the way into the chocolate. Lift
the berry above the chocolate and shake off the
excess, letting it drip back into the cup. Wipe a little
chocolate from 1 side of the berry very gently on
the edge of the cup. Set the berry on the lined cookie
sheet, wiped side down, and slide it forward slightly
to avoid a puddle forming at the tip. Refrigerate the
berries as soon as the first tray is filled. Do not keep
the berries for long at room temperature or the
chocolate will turn dull and streaky. Dip and refrigerate
the remaining berries. Berries are ready to serve as
soon as the chocolate is hardened; leave them in the
fridge until serving time. Transfer each to a fluted
paper cup, if desired.

Strawberry Basket for Mom: Serve chocolate-dipped
long-stemmed strawberries in a chocolate basket
(see page 70). If the berries are dipped in bittersweet
chocolate, make the basket with white or milk chocolate
for contrast.

white chocolate–lemon cheesecake

White chocolate gives an undertone of flavor to this rich but subtle lemon cheesecake with the best simple-to-do crunchy shortbread crust ever. Use a good-quality white chocolate, such as Callebaut, El Rey, Lindt, or Valrhona.

CRUST

8 tablespoons (1 stick) unsalted butter

1/4 cup sugar

1 teaspoon vanilla extract

1/8 teaspoon salt

1 cup all-purpose flour

FILLING

6 ounces white chocolate, finely chopped

1/4 cup boiling water

1 1/2 pounds cream cheese, at room temperature

1/2 cup plus 2 tablespoons sugar

1 1/2 teaspoons vanilla extract

2 teaspoons grated lemon zest

3 tablespoons strained fresh lemon juice

2 eggs, at room temperature

EQUIPMENT

8-inch springform pan, lightly greased

Position a rack in the lower third of the oven. Preheat the oven to 350°F.

To make the crust, cut the butter into chunks and melt it in a medium saucepan over low heat. Remove from the heat and stir in the sugar, vanilla, and salt. Add the flour and mix just until incorporated. Press the dough evenly over the bottom and about halfway up the sides of the pan. Bake until the crust is a rich golden brown and very brown at the edges, 20 to 25 minutes. Cool on a rack before filling. Grease the sides of the pan again, above the crust level, to prevent the filling from sticking to the pan above the crust.

Lower the oven temperature to 325°F.

To make the filling, place the white chocolate in a small bowl. Pour the boiling water over the chocolate and stir until smooth. Set aside.

In a medium mixing bowl, beat the cream cheese just until smooth, about 30 seconds. Scrape the bowl and beaters. Add the sugar, vanilla, lemon zest, and juice and beat just until smooth and creamy, 1 to 2 minutes. Add 1 egg and beat just until incorporated. Scrape the bowl and beaters. Beat in the second egg. Stir in the melted chocolate. Pour the batter into the prepared crust and smooth the top.

Bake until the edges of the cake are puffed but the center looks moist and jiggles when tapped, 35 to 40 minutes. Remove the cake from the oven. Slide the tip of a thin paring knife carefully around the top edge of the cake to detach it from the pan, but do not remove the pan sides. Place the pan on a rack and cover the pan and the rack with a large inverted bowl or pot so that the cake cools slowly. Cover and refrigerate the cooled cake at least 5 hours, preferably 24 hours, before serving.

apricot orange wedding cakes

Pretty cupcakes displayed on a tiered crystal or silver server are like an edible wedding bouquet. The cakes are easily doable at home, made in shifts or by more than one baker in more than one kitchen. A gathering of bridesmaids, friends, and dear ones of all ages to decorate the cupcakes will be a memorable celebration.

3/4 cup finely diced, moist dried apricots

4 tablespoons brandy

2 cups less 2 tablespoons all-purpose flour

3/8 teaspoon baking powder

3/8 teaspoon baking soda

3/8 teaspoon salt

3 eggs, at room temperature

1/2 cup buttermilk, at room temperature

Grated zest of 3/4 orange

1 1/2 teaspoons vanilla extract

12 tablespoons (1 1/2 sticks) unsalted butter, at room temperature

1 1/2 cups sugar

White Chocolate Glaze (page 82)

Edible flowers or petals, crystallized violets or rose petals, silver shot, gold leaf, etc. (optional)

EQUIPMENT

2 standard muffin tins, lined with fluted liners

Tiered pastry server

Combine the apricots with the brandy and let soak at least 15 minutes.

Position a rack in lower third of the oven. Preheat the oven to 325°F.

Mix together and sift the flour with the baking powder, baking soda, and salt. Set aside. Whisk the eggs with a fork to combine whites and yolks. Set aside.

Combine the apricots and brandy with the buttermilk, orange zest, and vanilla.

In a medium bowl with an electric mixer (using the flat beater or paddle instead of the whisk on heavy-duty stand mixers), beat the butter for a few seconds until creamy. Gradually add the sugar and continue to beat at medium to medium-high speed until light and fluffy, 3 to 4 minutes. Dribble in the eggs gradually and continue to beat for a total of about 2 minutes. Stop the mixer. Add one third of the flour mixture. Beat on low speed just until incorporated. Stop the mixer. Pour in half of the buttermilk mixture. Beat on low speed just until incorporated. Repeat with half the remaining flour followed by all of the remaining buttermilk, and finally the rest of the flour. Mix only until each addition is well incorporated. Divide the batter evenly among the lined muffin cups.

Bake until a toothpick inserted in the center of 2 or 3 cupcakes comes out clean, 20 to 25 minutes. Cool in the pans on a rack. *Cool completely before frosting or storing. Cupcakes keep well at room temperature for about 4 days or may be frozen up to 3 months.*

Frost with White Chocolate Glaze and decorate with a selection of edible fresh flowers or petals, crystallized rose petals or violets, silver or gold shot, or gold leaf, if desired.

white chocolate glaze

Use a good-quality white chocolate, such as Callebaut, El Rey, Lindt, or Valrhona. White chocolate varies among brands, so you may have to make small adjustments to the consistency of the frosting, as noted in the recipe. Consider this a normal part of life with white chocolate. (The recipe will not work with white chocolate chips.)

9 ounces good-quality white chocolate

¹/₄ cup heavy cream

1 tablespoon plus 1 teaspoon light corn syrup

1¹/₂ teaspoons grated orange zest (optional)

1¹/₂ teaspoons orange juice (optional)

Chop the chocolate very fine so that the largest pieces are no bigger than lentils, or pulverize it in a food processor. Transfer the chocolate to a medium bowl. Don't be tempted to complete the recipe in the processor, or the glaze will be hard as a rock once it cools.

Bring the cream and corn syrup to a boil. Immediately pour the hot cream over the chocolate and stir until the mixture is smooth and the chocolate is entirely melted. Stir in the orange zest and juice, if using. Cool at room temperature, without stirring, for at least 1 hour, or until ready to use.

If the mixture is creamy and spreadable and holds a nice soft shape, use a spatula to spread it on the cakes. If it has the consistency of very thick, slow-flowing honey, dip the cake tops directly into it (it will dry with a lovely translucent sheen). Or you can thicken it to a creamy spreadable frosting by beating it very briefly with a rubber spatula. Don't overdo it, or the glaze will harden after it sets. If it becomes too stiff to spread, warm the spatula in hot water and wipe it dry as you spread, or set the entire bowl in a larger bowl of hot water and stir until the mixture softens slightly. If it separates from overwarming, beat with the spatula just until it comes back together.

chocolate banana waffles for dad

My dad loves bananas—almost as much as he likes kippered herring. Chocolate doesn't go with herring, so here's the compromise I found that pleases everyone.

4 firm ripe bananas

10 tablespoons (1¼ sticks) unsalted butter

¼ cup plus 2 tablespoons (packed) brown sugar

Splash of rum (optional)

¾ cup all-purpose flour

2 tablespoons granulated sugar

2 teaspoons baking powder

¼ teaspoon salt

¼ cup unsweetened cocoa powder, natural or Dutch process

½ cup milk

½ teaspoon instant coffee powder

1 egg

½ teaspoon vanilla extract

1 cup crème fraîche, for serving

EQUIPMENT

Large skillet

Waffle iron

Cut the bananas in half lengthwise. Cut each half into 3 or 4 pieces. Heat 2 tablespoons of the butter in a large skillet. Sauté the banana pieces 3 to 5 minutes on each side, or until tender and browned. Sprinkle with 2 tablespoons of the brown sugar, turn once more, and splash with rum, if using. Set aside and reheat when the waffles are ready.

In a medium bowl, mix the flour, granulated sugar, baking powder, and salt. Set aside.

Melt the remaining 8 tablespoons of butter in a small saucepan. Stir in the cocoa until smooth and hot. Gradually stir in the milk until smooth. Off the heat, whisk in the remaining ¼ cup of brown sugar, coffee powder, egg, and vanilla, stirring until the mixture is completely smooth. Pour the contents of the saucepan over the flour mixture and stir until the dry ingredients are completely moistened.

Preheat the waffle iron. Make each waffle with ¼ to ⅓ cup of batter, cooking just until steam stops rising from the sides of the waffle iron. Either serve immediately topped with warm sautéed bananas and a dollop of crème fraîche, or cool very briefly on a rack to crisp before serving. Waffles may also be made in advance, cooled on a rack, and reheated on a cookie sheet in a 350°F. oven for a few minutes before serving.

Summer chocolate is quixotic. I sometimes aim for the simple satisfaction of a perfect Chocolate Pound Cake that's neither too rich nor too gooey to enjoy in sultry weather. But I like to tease and surprise the palate, too. I play with contrasting textures, temperatures, and flavors to wake up sleeping taste buds. Ice cream with warm chocolate sauce and tangy berries in crunchy caramel lace cups screams summer. Ditto Hot Waffle Ice Cream Sandwiches with *dolce de leche* ice cream. Chocolate-dipped frozen bananas are pure summer nostalgia to me, and I love the unexpected flavors in Mini Blackberry Caramel Cheesecakes. Summer chocolate is seductive!

independence day sundaes | Nut-and-caramel lace cookie cups filled with ice cream, berries, and chocolate sauce are perfect for a summer dinner party or a festive Fourth of July. Play a little by substituting hazelnuts, macadamias, pecans, or peanuts for the almonds.

COOKIES

2 teaspoons fresh lemon juice

5 tablespoons unsalted butter

2 tablespoons light corn syrup

3 tablespoons sugar

1 tablespoon all-purpose flour

1/2 teaspoon grated lemon zest

1/2 cup finely chopped almonds

FILLING

Vanilla ice cream, for serving

1 pint strawberries, rinsed, hulled, and halved or sliced

1 pint blueberries or blackberries, rinsed and patted dry

Chocolate Sauce, warm (page 88)

EQUIPMENT

2 heavy cookie sheets

2 custard cups

Position a rack in the center of oven. Preheat the oven to 350°F. Line each cookie sheet with a sheet of lightweight foil cut in half crosswise. Turn 2 custard cups upside down on the work surface. Cover each cup with a paper towel, tucked under the cup to secure it.

To make the cookies, in a small heavy saucepan, boil lemon juice until it is reduced to a glaze, about 1 minute. Reduce the heat to low. Add the butter, corn syrup, sugar, flour, and lemon zest and stir until the butter melts. Remove from the heat and stir in the almonds.

Drop 1 tablespoonful of batter into the center of each half sheet of foil. Bake until the batter spreads, bubbles, and turns deep caramel color, 8 to 10 minutes, rotating the sheets back to front about halfway through the baking time. Allow the cookies to cool just long enough (1 minute plus or minus 15 seconds) to set at the edges. Lift the foil sheets with the cookies attached and turn them upside down, one on each of the paper-draped cups. Using a pot holder, press the foil and cookie gently over the cup. There is no need to press hard or form deep cookie cups—shallow ones are just as pretty and less likely to break when filled with ice cream. Allow the cookies to cool before removing them from the inverted cups. Peel the foil away very gently. Set each cookie on a paper towel to absorb any extra butter, if necessary. Repeat with the remaining batter, baking 2 cookies at a time.

Transfer the cookies to an airtight container as soon as they are cool so that they will not soften or become sticky from the moisture in the air. The cookies will be very fragile; I usually make more than I need, just in case (the recipe makes 10 to 12 cookies).

To serve the sundaes, place a cookie cup on each plate and fill it carefully with a scoop of ice cream and some berries. Pass a pitcher of warm chocolate sauce.

chocolate sauce

I have always used this sauce. I throw it together whenever there is a chocolate sauce emergency (which tends to happen at my house); I also make it especially for company.

10 ounces bittersweet or semisweet chocolate, chopped into small pieces

1/2 to 3/4 cup milk, half-and-half, or heavy cream, or 1/2 to 3/4 cup milk plus 2 tablespoons butter

1/2 teaspoon vanilla extract

To make the sauce, in a small bowl, combine the chocolate and the lesser amount of liquid (and butter, if using) and melt gently in a barely simmering water bath or microwave on Medium (50 percent) power for about 2 minutes. Stir until smooth. Add more liquid if the sauce seems too thick or looks curdled, or if it hardens too much when tested over ice cream. Remove from the heat and stir in the vanilla. Use the warm sauce immediately, or set aside until needed and rewarm briefly. *The sauce keeps several days in the refrigerator.*

Note: The beauty of this recipe is that you can tailor it to your own taste and the type of chocolate you are using. I usually prefer my sauce made with milk (no butter) rather than half-and-half or cream because the chocolate flavor is most intense that way. For an even more intense chocolate experience, choose a bittersweet chocolate labeled anywhere from 66 to 72 percent; then you will need the larger amount of liquid called for to make the sauce adequately fluid. Since chocolates are all a little different, it's a good idea to test in the kitchen by spooning a little over ice cream and waiting a few seconds before tasting. If the sauce hardens too much on ice cream, add a little more liquid until it is just the way you like it.

boardwalk bananas

I grew up in a smoggy suburb of Los Angeles. Heaven in summer was a chocolate-dipped frozen banana and a barefoot stroll on the pier in Balboa Beach. The perfume of suntan lotion, fish trimmings, and a salty breeze complete the memory. Homemade chocolate coating improves that boardwalk banana, but nothing beats the memory.

6 to 8 firm ripe bananas

About 6 tablespoons (3/4 stick) unsalted butter, to make about 4 tablespoons clarified butter

10 ounces semisweet chocolate, cut into small pieces

1 cup chopped toasted almonds, peanuts, or hazelnuts, or chocolate jimmies

EQUIPMENT

6 to 8 disposable wooden chopsticks or Popsicle sticks

Bread pan or similar container

To prepare the bananas, cut away each banana's stem without removing the peel and push a chopstick 1 inch or more into the flesh. Then peel the bananas and freeze them. If not dipping right away, transfer them to an airtight container or zipper lock bag and return to the freezer.

To clarify the butter, cut the butter into pieces and put it in a 1-cup glass measure or a small glass jar. Set the glass in a pan of simmering water and heat, without stirring, until the butter is melted and hot and has separated into three layers: foamy milk solids on top, golden butter oil in the center, and a watery looking mixture on the bottom. Skim and discard the white foam. Spoon out and save the yellow oil (clarified butter) and discard the rest.

In the top of a double boiler or in a heatproof bowl set in a skillet of barely simmering water, combine the chocolate and 4 tablespoons of clarified butter. Stir until the chocolate is melted and smooth.

In order to dip each banana quickly and completely and only once into the chocolate (which will begin to harden immediately), you will need a banana-shaped trough. Place a large piece of heavy-duty foil loosely over a bread pan. Using the pan for support, mold the foil into a narrow trough, slightly wider than a banana and deep enough to submerge the whole fruit, held by the stick, with the curved side down. Pour the chocolate mixture into the trough.

Line a shallow pan with wax or parchment paper. Have the nuts or jimmies ready. Remove the bananas from the freezer. Holding the stick, dip a banana quickly and completely in and out of the chocolate. Hold it over the lined pan and sprinkle all sides with nuts or jimmies before the chocolate sets. Set the banana on the lined pan. Repeat with the remaining bananas. Transfer the bananas to the freezer to harden completely, then to an airtight container or zipper lock bag. Keep frozen until ready to serve. *Leftover coating may be frozen and used again.*

Note: To prepare bananas for a crowd, omit the foil trough. A triple or quadruple recipe of chocolate coating makes 33/4 or 5 cups and may be put in a container tall enough to dip the entire banana upside down. *Freeze leftover chocolate.*

mini blackberry caramel cheesecakes

These little cheesecakes are baked in caramel-lined cups just like flan. I experimented with lots of different variations, but I said, "Wow!" when I tasted the final version. Be sure to use good-quality white chocolate.

CARAMEL

1 cup sugar

1/2 cup water

CHEESECAKES

6 ounces white chocolate, finely chopped

1/4 cup boiling water

1 1/2 pounds cream cheese, at room temperature

1/2 cup plus 2 tablespoons sugar

1 1/2 teaspoons vanilla extract

2 eggs, at room temperature

5 ounces ripe blackberries, rinsed and patted dry

EQUIPMENT

8 five- or six-ounce ramekins or custard cups

Baking pan large enough to hold all of the cups

Position a rack in the lower third of the oven. Preheat the oven to 325°F.

To make the caramel, have a white plate and a skewer or spoon next to the stove to test the color of the syrup. In a 1-quart saucepan, combine the sugar and water. Stir (do not whisk) gently over medium heat until most of the sugar looks dissolved. Stop stirring and bring the mixture to a simmer. Cover and simmer 2 to 3 minutes to dissolve the sugar. Uncover and increase the heat to medium. Simmer without stirring (swirl the pot rather than stirring if it seems to be cooking unevenly) until the syrup begins to color. Using the skewer, drop a bead of syrup on the white plate. When a drop of syrup looks pale amber on the plate, pay close attention. Continue to cook until test drops darken to a slightly reddish amber color. Immediately pour an equal quantity of caramel into each ramekin. Tilt each cup to spread caramel over the bottom and partway up the sides. Set the cups aside to cool.

Put a full kettle of water on to boil.

To make the cheesecakes, place the chocolate in a small bowl. Pour the boiling water over the chocolate and stir until smooth. Set aside.

In a medium bowl, beat the cream cheese just until smooth, about 30 seconds. Scrape the bowl and beaters. Add the sugar and vanilla and beat just until smooth, 1 to 2 minutes. Add 1 egg and beat just until incorporated. Scrape the bowl and beaters. Beat in the second egg. Stir in the melted chocolate. Divide the berries among the caramelized cups, then divide the batter among the cups, pouring it on top of the berries.

Place the cups in the baking pan. Carefully pour boiling water into the baking pan to a depth of 1 inch. Bake until the edges of the cheesecakes are puffed but the centers still jiggle when the cups are tapped, 15 to 20 minutes. Remove the pan from the oven. Use tongs to transfer each cup from the hot water to a rack to cool completely. Cover and refrigerate the cheesecakes at least overnight, preferably longer, before serving. To unmold and serve, run a knife around the cheesecakes' edges and invert onto individual serving plates.

strawberry mocha meringue

SERVES 10

This flavor combination is surprising and delightful. For maximum crunch, serve shortly after assembling; for more blended flavors and textures, serve hours later. Instead of piping two layers for a single large dessert, you can form small meringue shells to make individual desserts.

WHITE CHOCOLATE CREAM

9 ounces white chocolate, finely chopped

1 1/2 cups heavy cream

MERINGUES

3 egg whites, at room temperature

1/8 teaspoon cream of tartar

3/4 cup sugar

2 teaspoons instant coffee or espresso powder

1 1/2 to 2 pints strawberries, rinsed, patted dry, hulled, and cut in half

EQUIPMENT

Large baking sheet, lined with parchment

Large pastry bag

Plain pastry tip with a 1/2-inch opening (Ateco #9806 or #806) and a medium or large star tip (Ateco #856 or #9826) (optional)

To make the white chocolate cream, place the chocolate in a medium bowl. In a small saucepan, bring the cream to a low boil. Pour the hot cream immediately over the chopped chocolate and stir gently until the chocolate is completely melted and smooth. Refrigerate several hours or up to 2 days.

Position a rack in the center of the oven. Preheat the oven to 200°F.

To make the coffee meringues, use a heavy pencil to trace two 8-inch circles, 1 inch apart, on the baking sheet liner. Turn the paper, pencil side down.

In a clean, dry mixer bowl, beat the egg whites and cream of tartar on medium speed until soft peaks form when the beaters are lifted. On high speed, gradually add half of the sugar and all the coffee powder, about 1 tablespoon at a time, taking 1 to 1 1/2 minutes. The mixture should stand in stiff glossy peaks when the beaters are lifted. Fold in the remaining sugar with a rubber spatula.

If using a pastry bag, insert the plain tip and scrape the meringue into the bag. Starting at the center of one circle, pipe an ever-widening spiral of meringue (counterclockwise if you are right-handed) to cover the entire circle. Repeat with the second circle. Or scrape half of the meringue into each circle and spread it evenly with a metal spatula.

Bake for 2 hours and allow to cool in a turned-off oven. Cool the meringues completely before using or storing. *Meringues may be stored in an airtight container at least 2 months.*

To assemble the dessert, set aside the best meringue for the top. With an electric mixer, beat the chilled white chocolate cream until it stiffens like thick whipped cream. Use a pastry bag fitted with a star tip to pipe about two thirds of the cream over the bottom meringue. Or use a metal spatula to spread it. Arrange the sliced berries over the cream. Spread or pipe the remaining cream over the berries to hold the top meringue; don't try to cover all of the berries. Set the top in place. Refrigerate until serving.

the new strawberries and cream

White chocolate and cream infused with fresh peppermint are a cool partner for ripe strawberries. Be sure to use a quality brand of white chocolate, such as Callebaut, El Rey, Lindt, or Valrhona. Do not use white chocolate chips or white coating made with vegetable fat instead of cocoa butter.

1 bunch fresh mint

1 cup heavy cream

8 ounces white chocolate, finely chopped

1 quart ripe strawberries

1/3 cup slivered or sliced almonds, toasted

EQUIPMENT   6 or 8 dessert dishes

To make the mint cream, rinse the mint and blot it dry with paper towels. Set aside 6 to 8 good-looking small sprigs to garnish the dishes. Chop enough of the remaining leaves to make 1/4 cup (lightly packed). Combine the chopped mint and cream in a small saucepan and bring to a boil. Remove the pot from the heat. Cover the pot and let the mint steep for 5 minutes.

Meanwhile, place the chocolate in a medium bowl and set a strainer across it. Pour the cream through the strainer, pressing on the mint to extract the cream. Discard the mint. Stir the chocolate mixture until perfectly smooth and melted. Refrigerate at least 4 hours or up to 2 days.

To serve, rinse the strawberries and pat them dry. Hull and cut the berries in halves or quarters and divide them among the dessert dishes. Beat the chilled white chocolate mixture with an electric mixer until the cream stiffens and holds a shape like thick whipped cream. Top each dish of berries with a dollop of mint cream, sprinkle with toasted almonds, and garnish with a sprig of mint.

chocolate pound cake | **SERVES 10**

This is my favorite perfectly plain chocolate cake. It needs no frosting or glaze. Take it on a picnic, nibble it for breakfast, or doll it up with fruit and cream, or ice cream and chocolate sauce. Double the recipe and store one cake in the freezer for unexpected guests.

1 cup all-purpose flour

1/2 cup unsweetened Dutch-process cocoa powder

1/4 teaspoon baking powder

Scant 1/4 teaspoon baking soda

Scant 1/2 teaspoon salt

1/2 cup buttermilk, at room temperature

1 teaspoon vanilla extract

2 teaspoons instant espresso or coffee powder

10 tablespoons (11/4 sticks) unsalted butter, at room temperature

11/3 cups granulated sugar

3 eggs, at room temperature

Powdered sugar, for dusting (optional)

EQUIPMENT 6-cup decorative tube pan, such as a Turk's Head or Kugelhopf pan, sprayed with vegetable oil spray

Position a rack in the lower third of the oven. Preheat the oven to 350°F.

To make the cake, whisk together and sift the flour, cocoa, baking powder, baking soda, and salt. Set aside.

Combine the buttermilk with the vanilla and espresso powder. Stir to dissolve the coffee. Set aside.

In a medium to large bowl, with an electric mixer (using the flat beater or paddle instead of the whisk on heavy-duty stand mixers), beat the butter for a few seconds until creamy. Add the granulated sugar in a steady stream and continue to beat at high speed with a hand-held mixer or medium speed with a stand mixer, until light and fluffy, 4 to 5 minutes. Meanwhile break the eggs into a cup and whisk them to combine the whites and yolks. Take a full 21/2 to 3 minutes to dribble the eggs gradually into the butter mixture, beating constantly.

Stop the mixer and add one third of the flour mixture. Beat on low speed only until no flour is visible. Stop the mixer and add half of the buttermilk mixture. Beat only until the liquid is absorbed. Repeat with half of the remaining flour mixture, then all of the remaining buttermilk, and finally the remaining flour. Stop the mixer each time you add ingredients and scrape the bowl as necessary. Beat on low speed only enough to incorporate ingredients after each addition. Scrape the batter into the pan and spread it evenly.

Bake until the cake starts to shrink away from the sides of the pan and a toothpick inserted in the center comes out dry, 40 to 45 minutes. Cool the cake in the pan on a rack 10 minutes before unmolding. Invert and cool the cake completely on a rack before wrapping or storing. Cake can be prepared to this point, wrapped well, and kept at room temperature. *Cake will remain moist and delicious for 4 to 5 days, or it may be frozen for up to 3 months.* Sieve powdered sugar over cake just before serving, if desired.

white chocolate–banana nectarine trifle

Never trifle with a trifle at the last minute because the flavors and textures always improve after a night in the fridge. Simply layer the ingredients as described, or set your inner artist free to cut and arrange the cake (an amazing no-fail genoise) and fillings more creatively.

CAKE

2/3 cup all-purpose flour

4 eggs, separated, at room temperature

1/4 teaspoon cream of tartar

2/3 cup sugar

1 teaspoon vanilla extract

3 tablespoons melted butter, warm

FILLING

2 cups heavy cream

1 teaspoon vanilla extract

3 to 4 teaspoons sugar

2 ripe bananas

4 medium-size ripe nectarines or peaches, or about 3 cups blackberries, or a combination, rinsed and patted dry

1/4 cup rum, or to taste

1/4 cup apricot or blackberry preserves

3 cups White Chocolate Custard Sauce (page 99), chilled

1/3 cup slivered or chopped almonds, toasted

EQUIPMENT

9-inch square pan, lined with parchment paper

2- or 3-quart trifle bowl or any attractive glass bowl

Plastic squeeze bottle or pastry brush (optional)

Pastry bag and star tip (optional)

Position a rack in the lower third of the oven. Preheat the oven to 350°F.

To make the cake, sift the flour and return it to the sifter. In a large bowl, beat the egg whites and cream of tartar at medium speed until soft peaks form when the beaters are lifted. Increase to high speed and add the sugar gradually, taking about 2 minutes. Beat in the vanilla and egg yolks. Sift half of the flour into the bowl and beat on low speed just until incorporated. Repeat with the remaining flour. Add the warm melted butter and beat just until evenly mixed. Scrape the batter into the pan and smooth the top.

Bake just until a toothpick inserted into the center comes out clean, 20 to 25 minutes. Cool on a wire rack at least 10 minutes before unmolding. To unmold, slide a slim knife around the cake, pressing against the sides of the pan to avoid tearing. Invert the cake onto a rack and peel off the parchment paper. Turn the cake right side up to cool completely.

In a chilled bowl with chilled beaters, whip the cream, vanilla, and sugar until nearly stiff. Refrigerate.

Peel and slice or cube the bananas and nectarines.

Cut the cake into 1/2-inch strips (or any shape). Arrange half of the strips in the bottom of the bowl. Drizzle or brush on half of the rum. Spread with half of the preserves. Pour half of the custard over the cake and cover with half of the fruit. Spread or pipe one third of the whipped cream over the fruit. Repeat with the remaining cake, rum, preserves, custard, and fruit. Pipe or dollop the remaining cream on top. Cover with an inverted bowl to avoid damaging the cream. Refrigerate overnight. Sprinkle with toasted almonds before serving.

white chocolate custard sauce | Use a quality white chocolate such as Callebaut, El Rey, Lindt, Valrhona, or Tobler. Do not use chips or morsels or white coatings, which are not made with real cocoa butter.

2 cups milk

6 egg yolks

6 tablespoons sugar

1 teaspoon vanilla extract

6 ounces white chocolate, finely chopped

EQUIPMENT

Heatproof silicon spatula (optional)

Instant-read thermometer, if you are not used to making custard sauce

To make the sauce, place a strainer over a clean bowl near the stove for the finished custard.

In a heavy-bottomed saucepan, heat the milk until it steams and tiny bubbles form around the edge of the pot.

Meanwhile, in another bowl, whisk the egg yolks and sugar until lightened in color. When the milk is ready, remove the pan from the heat and gradually whisk about one third of the milk into the egg-yolk mixture. Scrape back into the remaining hot milk and cook over low heat, stirring constantly with a heatproof spatula, if possible, or a wooden spoon, sweeping all over the sides and bottom of the pot, to prevent scorching. Cook slowly, stirring, until the custard has thickened to the consistency of heavy cream and the temperature does not exceed 170°F. Immediately scrape the custard into the strainer over the bowl and let drain. Remove the strainer and stir the vanilla into the bowl of custard. Cool the custard to lukewarm.

Once the custard is lukewarm, place the white chocolate in a clean, dry heatproof bowl large enough to eventually hold all of the custard. Melt the chocolate gently in the microwave on Low (30 percent) power for 3 to 4 minutes, stirring 2 or 3 times. Or set the bowl in a skillet of hot but not even simmering water, with the burner turned off, and stir the chocolate constantly until it is melted and smooth. Remove from the heat. Gradually stir the lukewarm custard sauce into the melted chocolate. Be sure not to stir the chocolate into the custard. Refrigerate until needed.

hot waffle ice cream sandwiches

Forget vanilla ice cream. Our favorite fillings for these sandwiches turned out to be either *dolce de leche* or coffee ice cream. Butter pecan is another winner.

3/4 cup all-purpose flour

2 tablespoons granulated sugar

2 teaspoons baking powder

1/4 teaspoon salt

8 tablespoons (1 stick) unsalted butter

1/4 cup unsweetened cocoa powder, natural or Dutch process

1/2 cup milk

1/4 cup (packed) brown sugar

1/2 teaspoon instant coffee powder

1 egg

1/2 teaspoon vanilla extract

1 pint *dolce de leche* or coffee ice cream

EQUIPMENT   Waffle iron

To make the waffles, in a medium bowl, mix the flour, granulated sugar, baking powder, and salt. Set aside.

Melt the butter in a small saucepan. Stir in the cocoa until smooth and hot. Gradually stir in the milk. Off the heat, whisk in the brown sugar, coffee powder, egg, and vanilla, stirring until the mixture is completely smooth. Pour over the flour mixture and stir until the dry ingredients are completely moistened.

Preheat the waffle iron. Make each waffle with 1/4 to 1/2 cup of batter (amount depends on your waffle iron), cooking just until steam stops rising from the sides of the iron. Place the cooked waffles on a rack to cool slightly and crisp.

Make the sandwiches while the waffles are still warm, or let the waffles cool and reheat them in a 350°F. oven for a few minutes before serving. To serve, press a scoop of ice cream between 2 waffle sections.

hazelnut chocolate meringue with blackberries

In northern California fabulous blackberries can often be had right up to Labor Day. I celebrate the last days of summer with a backyard barbecue and this informal dessert.

MERINGUE

5 ounces bittersweet or semisweet chocolate, chopped, or 3/4 cup semisweet chocolate chips

1/2 cup hazelnuts, toasted, skinned, and chopped medium fine

2/3 cup sugar

3 egg whites

1/8 teaspoon cream of tartar

FILLING

1 cup heavy cream

1/2 teaspoon vanilla extract

1 tablespoon sugar

1 1/2 pints blackberries, rinsed and spread out to dry on paper towels

EQUIPMENT

Baking sheet, lined with parchment paper

Pastry bag

Plain pastry tip with a 1/2-inch opening (Ateco #806 or #807) (optional)

Position a rack in the center of the oven. Preheat the oven to 300°F.

To make the chocolate meringue, using a heavy pencil line, trace one 9-inch circle or a 12x6-inch rectangle or any other shape of similar size on the baking sheet liner. Turn the paper over so that pencil marks will not transfer to the meringue.

Mix the chocolate with the nuts and half of the sugar. Set aside.

In a clean, dry mixing bowl, beat the egg whites and cream of tartar on medium speed until soft peaks form when the beaters are lifted. On high speed, gradually add the remaining sugar, about a tablespoon at a time, taking 1 to 1 1/2 minutes. The mixture should stand in stiff glossy peaks when the beaters are lifted. Use a rubber spatula to fold in the chocolate mixture, just until incorporated. If you are using a pastry bag, insert the plain round tip and scrape the meringue into the bag. Starting at the center of the traced circle, pipe an ever-widening spiral of meringue (counter-clockwise if you are right-handed) to cover the entire circle. Pipe a raised border around the edge. Or scrape the meringue into the center of the traced circle. With the back of a large spoon, spread the meringue to form a shallow shell with slightly raised edges.

Bake 10 to 15 minutes, or until the meringue begins to turn golden. Turn the oven down to 200°F. and continue to bake for 2 hours. Cool the meringue in a turned-off oven. Cool completely before using or storing. *Meringues may be stored in an airtight container at least 2 months.*

To make the filling, in a chilled bowl with chilled beaters, beat the cream with the vanilla and sugar until nearly stiff. Fill the meringue shell with the whipped cream. Mound the berries on top. Refrigerate until serving.

fastest fudge cake

SERVES 8 TO 10

Here's an emergency foolproof birthday or summer supper cake too good to save for an emergency. Don't even look for the mixer. I get the best results stirring with a rubber spatula or a wooden spoon. For speed, melt the butter in a large microwave-safe mixing bowl to eliminate a dirty pot and make the frosting while the cake bakes.

1 cup all-purpose flour

1/4 cup plus 2 tablespoons unsweetened natural cocoa powder

1/2 teaspoon baking soda

1/4 teaspoon salt

8 tablespoons (1 stick) melted unsalted butter, warm

1 1/4 cups (packed) brown sugar

2 eggs, cold or at room temperature

1 teaspoon vanilla extract

1/2 cup hot tap water

Fast Fudge Frosting (page 105)

EQUIPMENT   8-inch square or 9-inch round cake pan

Position a rack in the lower third of the oven. Grease the bottom of the pan or line it with parchment paper. Preheat the oven to 350°F.

To make the cake, whisk the flour, cocoa, baking soda, and salt together. Sift only if the cocoa remains lumpy. Set aside.

In a large bowl, combine the warm melted butter and brown sugar. Add the eggs and vanilla and stir until well blended. Add all of the flour mixture at once. Using a rubber spatula or wooden spoon, stir only until all the flour is moistened. Pour the hot water over the batter all at once. Stir only until the water is incorporated and the batter is smooth. Scrape the batter into the pan.

Bake until a toothpick inserted in the center of the cake comes out clean, 25 to 30 minutes. Cool the cake in the pan on a rack for about 10 minutes before unmolding. To unmold, slide a slim knife around the edges of the cake to release it from the pan. Invert the cake and peel off the paper liner. Turn the cake right side up and cool it completely on a rack before frosting the top and sides. Or cool the cake in the pan and frost the top only.

fast fudge frosting It's not only fast, it's versatile. Serve it warm over ice cream for a great sauce, dip cupcake tops in it, or pour it over a pound cake.

5 tablespoons unsalted butter

³/₄ cup sugar

²/₃ cup unsweetened cocoa powder

Pinch of salt

³/₄ cup heavy cream

1 teaspoon vanilla extract

In a medium saucepan, melt the butter. Stir in the sugar, cocoa, and salt. Gradually stir in the cream. Heat, stirring constantly, until the mixture is smooth and hot but not boiling. Remove from the heat and stir in the vanilla. Cool until thickened to the consistency of frosting, or use warm for a glaze or sauce. *Store leftover frosting in the refrigerator. Rewarm gently in a pan of barely simmering water or in a microwave before using.*

dressing up desserts

tempering chocolate

ingredients

equipment

resources

index

dressing up desserts

The best decorations for any dessert are simple, elegant, and edible. While it is customary to match flavors—using peanut brittle to decorate a peanut butter layer cake or caramel-glazed hazelnuts or almonds on a hazelnut or almond cake—chocolate shavings and curls are at home almost anywhere, as are gold and silver.

SIMPLE CHOCOLATE SHAVINGS

For fine shavings, scrape the blade of a sharp knife against the flat side of a bar of chocolate. Use a metal spatula to scoop them up; they will melt instantly from the warmth of your hands. For thicker, larger shavings, let the bar of chocolate warm up gradually in a warm corner of the kitchen and rub it with the heel of your hand. Or set the chocolate under a desk lamp to soften it ever so slightly without melting it. Hold the knife blade at a 90-degree angle to the chocolate and scrape toward you while anchoring the bar with your other hand. Milk and white chocolate are softer than dark chocolate, so they yield larger shavings and curls, with less warming.

PERFECT CHOCOLATE CURLS

This easy recipe makes picture-perfect chocolate curls.

INGREDIENTS

6 ounces semisweet or bittersweet chocolate, finely chopped
1 1/2 teaspoons clarified butter or 1 tablespoon vegetable shortening

EQUIPMENT

Small loaf pan, lined with plastic wrap

Place the chocolate and clarified butter in a small heatproof bowl in a pan of barely simmering water. Stir constantly until the mixture is melted and smooth.

Scrape the chocolate into the pan. Chill at least 2 hours, or until firm. Lift the plastic wrap to remove the chocolate. Let stand 10 to 15 minutes to soften the chocolate slightly. Cut the chocolate lengthwise to form 2 long bars no wider than the cutting blade of your vegetable peeler. Scrape the chocolate firmly with the peeler for curls and cigarette shapes. If curls splinter or crack, wait a few more minutes and try again. If chocolate becomes too soft, return it to the refrigerator to harden. Handle chocolate curls with a toothpick to avoid fingerprints. *Store curls in the refrigerator, tightly covered, or freeze.*

CHOCOLATE PIPING AND CHOCOLATE LEAVES

For fine scrollwork borders on cakes, writing happy birthday, or making chocolate leaves, nothing beats the elegance, ease, and taste of pure melted chocolate. Use bar chocolate, rather than chocolate chips, which do not melt well. Finely chop 2 to 3 ounces of chocolate (dark chocolate, milk chocolate, or white chocolate) and place it in a clean, dry heatproof bowl. Fill a skillet with about 1 inch of water and bring it to a gentle simmer.

To melt semisweet or bittersweet chocolate, set the bowl of chocolate in the skillet and stir until melted and smooth. Or microwave on Medium (50 percent) power for 1 1/2 to 2 1/2 minutes, stirring from time to time, just until the chocolate is melted and smooth.

To melt white or milk chocolate, remove the skillet from the heat and wait 30 seconds before setting the bowl of chocolate in it. Stir constantly until the chocolate is melted. Or microwave on Low (30 percent) power for $1^1/_2$ to $2^1/_2$ minutes, stirring from time to time, until the chocolate is melted and smooth.

FOR PIPING

Scrape the chocolate into a small disposable plastic decorating bag or the corner of a zipper lock plastic bag. Close the bag and gather the excess in your fist, pushing the chocolate into the corner. Snip off the tip and pipe the chocolate directly onto the cake or dessert. If the chocolate in the bag begins to harden as you work, microwave on Low (30 percent) power for 10 seconds at a time until the chocolate is warm and flowing again.

FOR CHOCOLATE LEAVES

Use nontoxic leaves with well-defined veins on the underside. Citrus and camellia leaves are favorites. Rinse and dry each leaf on both sides. Use a dinner knife or small spatula to spread a medium-thick coating of melted chocolate over the back (veined) side of each leaf. Spread the chocolate evenly over the leaf, a little thicker over the center vein. Use a finger to wipe chocolate from the edges of the leaf. Refrigerate the leaf, chocolate side up, until hardened. To unmold, peel the leaf very gently away from the chocolate. Keep the chocolate leaves refrigerated. Always prepare extra chocolate leaves in case of breakage.

GOLD AND SILVER

All that glitters on desserts is gold—real gold and silver. Silver shot as well as gold for decorating cakes and cookies are available in myriad sizes, along with gold- and silver-covered almonds (called dragées). But it is even more exciting to gild nuts or berries, chocolate leaves or curls, even caramel decorations with edible (be sure to check) 22- or 23-carat gold leaf or gold or silver petal dust (lustre dust).

GOLD LEAF

Gold leaf comes in individual sheets or books of sheets $3^1/_4$ inches square. Each sheet is infinitesimally thin and backed by a piece of tissue paper. Lift pieces of gold from the backing by touching the gold with a tiny, dry artist's brush (ask at an art supply store) or the point of a paring knife. The gold will stick to the brush or knifepoint. Then touch the gold to whatever you are gilding. Do not work in a draft or breathe heavily while working. It takes practice to get perfect control, but perfection is not essential for beautiful results.

GOLD AND SILVER POWDER

Also called petal dust or luster dust, powder is a little easier to control. Either simply brush it on with a dry brush or dissolve $1/_2$ teaspoon of powder by adding vodka one drop at a time, stirring with a tiny brush, until it is the consistency of paint. Add a drop of vodka as necessary as the "paint" evaporates.

STENCILS

Handmade stencils add a distinctive finish to simple desserts and eliminate the need for frosting. Use your imagination and a pair of scissors.

Fold paper and cut your own doilies. Ask kids to cut snowflakes or paper dolls. Unfold the paper and iron it to flatten. Paper stencils can be used several times. More permanent (and dirt-resistant) stencils can be cut with an X-acto knife from a sheet of Mylar or acetate from the art or office supply store. Found objects, such as maple leaves, pieces of fern, or anything else with an appealing silhouette, make great stencils too. Lay the item on the cake and sieve a very fine shower of cocoa or powdered sugar over it. Then lift and discard the item. One chef I know lays a crossed knife and fork on top of a cake before dusting it.

CARAMEL DECORATIONS

Shards of clear sparkling amber, brilliant nut brittle, jewel-like glazed nuts, and gossamer spun sugar are the glitz of the dessert world. And caramel is easy to make.

Store caramel decorations in an airtight container between double sheets of wax paper. To keep the caramel from getting moist and sticky, enclose a desiccant such as silica gel in the container (see page 124).

CARAMEL SHARDS AND SHAPES

Have ready a foil- or parchment-lined baking sheet and an oiled knife or oiled cookie cutter.

Prepare Basic Caramel (page 111). Immediately pour the hot caramel onto the foil-lined pan, tilting to spread. As soon as the caramel begins to harden, cut out as many shapes as possible with an oiled knife or oiled cookie cutter. For shards, let the caramel cool and harden completely without cutting. Cut and break into shards.

CARAMEL-GLAZED NUTS

Have ready a pan of ice water and a cake or bread pan.

Impale 30 to 40 walnut or pecan halves or whole hazelnuts or almonds (blanched or with skins) on thin wooden barbecue skewers.

Prepare Basic Caramel (page 111). As soon as test drops of syrup are slightly reddish amber, set the saucepan immediately into the ice water to stop the cooking and prevent the caramel from continuing to darken. Remove the caramel from the ice bath and tilt the pan at a 45-degree angle. Dip the skewered nuts, one by one, into the hot caramel and prop them up on the edge of the cake or bread pan. When the caramel glaze is cool and hardened, snip off any caramel drips or tails with a pair of scissors.

NUT BRITTLE

Have ready 1/2 cup small to medium whole nuts or pieces, such as chopped walnuts or pecans, toasted almonds, toasted and skinned hazelnuts, or lightly salted dry-roasted peanut halves. Have ready a foil- or parchment-lined baking sheet.

Prepare Basic Caramel (page 111) up to the point where the syrup looks light amber on the white plate. Add the nuts and turn them gently with a clean, dry wooden spoon or silicone spatula just until they are completely coated with syrup. Continue to cook, without stirring, until a drop of syrup looks deep reddish amber on the white plate. Immediately scrape the mixture onto the foil and spread as thin as possible. Let cool and harden. Break into shards or chop coarse.

SPUN SUGAR

Have ready a pan of ice water and a wire whisk altered by cutting each wire before it begins to bend back toward the handle, or several skewers in lieu of the whisk.

To make spun sugar from scratch, prepare Basic Caramel. As soon as test drops of syrup are slightly reddish amber, set the saucepan immediately into the ice water to stop the cooking and prevent the caramel from continuing to darken. Let the caramel cool until it is very thick and sticky.

Or, to make spun sugar from leftover caramel hardened in the bottom of a saucepan, heat the caramel very gently and slowly without simmering over very low heat until most of it is melted into a very thick sticky syrup; it is not necessary for all of the caramel to be completely melted.

Dip the ends of the snipped whisk, or the fanned skewers, into the hot sticky caramel and lift it about 12 inches above the pot. The caramel will thicken as it cools. At first it will flow from the wire tips in very fine threads. The caramel must cool a bit more before it is ready to spin. Continue to dip and lift the whisk repeatedly, watching the threads. Caramel is ready to spin when the threads become slightly thicker and more golden and flow more slowly. You will be able to grasp the threads in your bare hand, and pull them aside, stretching. Threads of caramel are not hot but the caramel in the container is *very* hot and so are all the droplets and thick globs that fall from the skewers or whisk. Each time you dip into the caramel, hold the whisk or skewers high and wait until the heaviest flow of caramel subsides into threads before you touch it. Pull the threads aside immediately, out from under the whisk so that any drops of caramel that fall cannot burn you. Continue to dip and wait for the threads, pulling them aside and onto the dessert. If the caramel gets too cool to spin, reheat gently over very low heat, without boiling. Spun sugar lasts a very short time. Serve immediately.

BASIC CARAMEL

1/2 cup sugar
1/4 cup water
1/8 teaspoon cream of tartar

Gather the equipment and other ingredients needed for making shards, glazed nuts, brittle, or spun sugar, before preparing the basic caramel. Have a white plate and a skewer or spoon at the side of the stove to test the color of the syrup.

In a 3- to 4-cup saucepan, combine the sugar, water, and cream of tartar. Stir gently (do not whisk) over medium heat until most of the sugar looks dissolved. Stop stirring and bring the mixture to a simmer. Cover and simmer 2 to 3 minutes to dissolve the sugar. Uncover and wash down the insides of the pot with a wet pastry brush or a wet wad of paper towel. Continue to simmer until the syrup begins to color. Swirl the pot rather than stirring it if the syrup seems to be coloring unevenly. Use the skewer to drop a bead of syrup on the white plate. When a drop of syrup looks pale amber on the plate, pay close attention. Continue to cook and test drops of syrup until they are darkened to a slightly reddish amber color. Proceed immediately with one of the preceding preparations.

tempering chocolate

Tempering chocolate involves a sequence of heating, stirring, and cooling steps that stabilize the cocoa-butter (fat) crystals and ensure that the chocolate dries shiny and hard and breaks with a snap instead of appearing gray or streaky with a soft cakey texture. Chocolate is always tempered by the manufacturer, so the bar that you buy is already tempered unless heat or moisture has damaged it.

Each time chocolate is melted, it must be tempered again if it is to dry glossy and crisp. There is no need to temper chocolate if it will be used as an ingredient in a batter or dessert, but tempered chocolate is usually necessary for molding and candy dipping. Choose good-tasting chocolate. Do not use chocolate chips or chocolate coatings that are not truly chocolate. Do not work in a hot room. Before tempering, prepare whatever is to be dipped and have it at room temperature. Measure out any other ingredients needed and have them at room temperature so that you can use the tempered chocolate as soon as it is ready. Do not allow any moisture to come in direct contact with the chocolate; resist the temptation to hurry the process with extra heat; and don't be too lazy to chop the chocolate as fine as directed. Make sure that the inside of the bowl, the spatula, and the thermometer stem are all clean and dry. Whenever you take the temperature of the chocolate or the water, wipe the stem clean or dry with a piece of paper towel.

Finally, and perhaps most important before you begin, remember that tempering is a function of three interrelated factors: time, temperature, and agitation. Although the temperature requirement is usually the focus of most instructions, time and stirring are equally important. This means that after following all of the steps

religiously to get your chocolate to the correct temperature, it may not *yet* be tempered. This is not failure. It usually means that the time and agitation requirements have not yet been met; stirring a little longer usually does the trick. The Test for Temper (page 113) is an essential form of feedback along the way.

TEMPERED CHOCOLATE

This particular tempering method requires that you begin with solid chocolate that is already in temper—nice shiny bars that are in the same condition that they were in when they left the chocolate factory. You may temper any amount of chocolate you like, using the following guidelines. Do not be concerned about tempering more chocolate than you need for a recipe or project; leftover tempered chocolate can be reused, or eaten.

INGREDIENTS

1 1/4 pounds solid tempered chocolate—semisweet, bittersweet, milk chocolate, or white chocolate

EQUIPMENT

Heatproof bowl with a 3- to 4-quart capacity, preferably stainless steel

Rubber spatula

Instant-read thermometer

A portable fan (optional)

Set aside one fifth of the total amount of chocolate in one or two large pieces. Chop the remaining chocolate into small pieces (1/2 inch or smaller) and place them in the bowl.

Warm the chocolate slowly so that it registers only about 100°F. by the time it is entirely melted, as follows: Set the bowl in a large skillet of barely simmering water and stir frequently at first, and then constantly until about three quarters of the chocolate is melted. Remove the chocolate from the heat and stir for 1 to 2 minutes. If the chocolate is not entirely melted, replace the bowl in the skillet and continue to stir.

Remove the chocolate from the heat. If the temperature exceeds 100°F., stir the chocolate to cool it to 100°F. Drop the reserved chunks of chocolate into the bowl and stir them around in the warm chocolate until the chocolate registers 90°F. for dark chocolate or 88°F. for white or milk chocolate. *(As you stir, you are cooling the melted chocolate and simultaneously melting the surface of the tempered chocolate chunks. As the temperature of the melted chocolate approaches 90°F., stable cocoa butter crystals from the surface of the chunks mingle with the melted chocolate and create more stable crystals. When there are enough stable crystals, the chocolate is tempered. The object is not to melt the chunks completely, but to use them to provide the necessary stable crystals for tempering the chocolate.)*

When the chocolate is at the desired temperature, it may or may not yet be tempered. Use The Test for Temper (at right). If the chocolate is in temper, use it immediately. If it is not in temper, continue to stir a few minutes longer, then test again. When the chocolate is in temper, remove the unmelted chunk(s) and set them aside on wax paper in the refrigerator for 10 minutes (then store at room temperature to be used again). Use the tempered chocolate immediately.

If you are using the chocolate for dipping, stir it from time to time and scrape the bowl to prevent chocolate from building up around the sides. The chocolate will cool and thicken as you work. You can set the bowl in hot water for a few seconds at a time and stir until the chocolate regains fluidity, so long as you do not exceed a maximum temperature of 91°F. for dark chocolate or 88°F. for milk and white chocolate. Or you can keep the bowl in a container of warm water just 2 degrees warmer than the maximum temperature of the type of chocolate you are working with. If the temperature of the chocolate exceeds the maximums, the stable crystals may be melted and destroyed and the chocolate will no longer be in temper. If that happens, add a new chunk of chocolate and stir until the chocolate is again in temper.

Leftover tempered chocolate can be scraped out onto a sheet of wax paper or foil and allowed to harden; wrap and store for another use.

THE TEST FOR TEMPER

Drizzle some chocolate on a knife blade or a piece of wax paper. Set the test in front of a fan (preferably) or in the refrigerator. If the chocolate starts to set within 3 minutes in front of the fan or in the refrigerator and dries hard without streaks or dulling, it is tempered. If it remains soft and wet looking after 3 minutes, it is not tempered.

ingredients

BAKING POWDER AND BAKING SODA

Cakes are sometimes leavened with baking powder or baking soda or both. Be sure that baking powder is fresh and stored in a tightly sealed container. If in doubt, splurge on a new tin.

BUTTER

I use unsalted butter for baking because it tastes better than shortening or margarine. Salted butter contains 1/4 teaspoon of salt per stick, which makes many butter-rich chocolate desserts taste much too salty. If using salted butter in a recipe where butter is a relatively minor ingredient, subtract 1/4 teaspoon of salt for each stick of salted butter used.

If you are baking for Jewish holidays and are strictly observing dietary laws, substitute unsalted pareve margarine for butter for nondairy meals. If you must use margarine or shortening instead of butter, avoid tub margarine, butter substitutes, and spreads, which may contain a very high percentage of water. These ingredients are not made for baking, and results will be unpredictable. You also cannot expect predictable results from substituting vegetable oils for solid fats.

COFFEE AND ESPRESSO

I use instant espresso powder from Medaglia D'Oro when espresso powder is called for. To substitute regular instant coffee powder or freeze-dried instant, use 25 to 30 percent more than the recipe calls for. If a recipe calls for freshly ground fresh coffee beans, use freshly roasted beans from a gourmet coffee purveyor and, preferably, grind them yourself. Bypass the vacuum-packed can of ground coffee from the supermarket.

CREAM

The best cream is simply pasteurized, rather than ultra-pasteurized or sterilized, and it contains no additional ingredients. The flavor is pure and fresh and clean. Buy it if you can. It is not easily available in all parts of the country because the ultra-pasteurized and sterilized products have a conveniently long shelf life. Unfortunately they also have a cooked or canned milk flavor.

DRIED FRUITS

These should be moist, plump, and flavorful. Whole pieces are always better, fresher, and moister than prechopped or extruded pellets, even if you have to chop your own. Use an oiled knife or oiled scissors to cut or chop sticky fruit.

EGGS

Use large grade AA eggs for the recipes in this book. Buy eggs from a source that keeps them refrigerated, and do likewise at your house. When recipes call for eggs at room temperature, remove them from the refrigerator an hour or so beforehand or bring them to room temperature quickly in a bowl of warm water.

EXTRACTS

Use pure extracts. Artificial flavorings are not worthy of the other good ingredients, and the time that you put into your favorite recipes. Almond extract is an exception. Pure almond extract (made with bitter almonds) is toxic in larger quantities. This means that pure almond extract is generally not available in the United States.

FLOUR

The recipes in this collection were tested and developed with bleached all-purpose flour, or cake flour where called for. The type of flour and method of measurement can make a critical difference in the outcome of cakes and desserts. See pages xiv–xix for the details that make a difference.

LIQUEURS AND SPIRITS

When recipes call for spirits, such as brandy or rum, use a brand that you can sip without grimacing. It is not necessary to use the finest or most expensive. I do not use liquor flavorings or extracts, because they taste artificial. It is almost always possible to omit the liqueur or spirits without making any other changes in a recipe.

NUTS

For freshness and flavor, buy nuts raw, rather than toasted, and in bulk from stores that have lots of turnover, rather than packaged from the supermarket. Larger halves and pieces stay fresher longer, so it's better to chop them yourself. Nuts keep well in the freezer, packaged airtight.

Fresh nuts are delicious raw, but toasting brings out such rich new flavors that almonds and hazelnuts are virtually transformed. Toasted nuts are also extra crunchy.

To toast nuts, spread them in a single layer on an ungreased cookie sheet. Bake in a preheated oven (350°F. for almonds and hazelnuts; 325°F. for pecans and walnuts) for 10 to 20 minutes, depending on the type of nut and whether they are whole, sliced, or slivered. Check the color and flavor of the nuts frequently, and stir to redistribute them on the pan. Almonds and hazelnuts are done when they are golden brown when you bite or cut them in half. To rub the bitter skins from toasted hazelnuts, cool them and then rub the nuts together until most of the skins flake off. Pecans and walnuts are done when fragrant and lightly colored.

When chopped toasted nuts are called for, toast them whole or in large pieces, let them cool, and then chop them.

To pulverize or grind nuts in a food processor without making paste or nut butter, start with a perfectly dry processor bowl and blade and nuts at room temperature. (Frozen or cold nuts will produce moisture that turns the nuts to paste, as will nuts still hot from the oven.) Use short pulses, stopping from time to time to scrape the corners of the processor bowl with a skewer or chopstick. If you observe these rules, there is no particular need to add some flour or sugar from the recipe to the nuts to keep them dry, although you may do so.

SPICES

For the best and brightest flavors, use pure extracts, real cinnamon, freshly grated nutmeg, and spices that still smell potent in the bottle.

SUGAR

I am increasingly convinced that cane sugar is preferable to beet sugar for baking and dessert making. All of the recipes in this book were tested with C&H cane sugar—granulated, golden (light) brown, or dark brown—purchased in the supermarket. Avoid sugar that contains fructose when baking cakes.

Granulated sugar seems to vary in coarseness in different parts of the country. Coarse sugar makes cookies tough and may affect the texture of cakes as well. If your sugar is coarser than regular table salt and/or your cookies are tough and cakes don't always rise, switch to C&H Baker's Sugar, bar sugar, fine granulated sugar, or even superfine sugar, or simply process your regular granulated sugar briefly in the food processor before using it.

Powdered sugar, also called confectioners' sugar or icing sugar, is granulated sugar that has been pulverized and mixed with a little cornstarch to prevent clumping. I use powdered sugar mostly for dusting—sieved over desserts or cookies for the visual effect. I rarely mix powdered sugar into batters or doughs because I do not like the flavor of the starch.

Golden (light) brown and dark brown sugars impart wonderful caramel or butterscotch flavor to desserts. I usually specify my preference for light or dark brown sugar, but you may use them interchangeably.

Measure brown sugar by packing it fairly firmly into the measuring cup. Brown sugar should be lump free before it is added to a batter or dough; it is unlikely to smooth out after it is added. Soft lumps can be squeezed with your fingers or mashed with a fork before adding. If the brown sugar is quite hard or has hard lumps, process it in a food processor or push it through a strainer. If you soften the sugar by warming it, the warm sugar may cause the batter to separate or curdle.

Save lumpy sugar and warmed sugar to top your oatmeal or use it to make applesauce or something where lumps do not matter.

chocolate and cocoa for baking and dessert making

CHOOSING BRANDS OF CHOCOLATE

Buy chocolate that you like and can afford. The recipes in this book will work and will taste fine made with baking chocolate, readily available in the grocery store, which is conveniently divided into individually wrapped 1- or 2-ounce portions. However, great chocolate makes especially delicious chocolate desserts. I urge you to taste and try quality bar chocolate made for baking and eating, such as Callebaut, Michel Cluizel, E. Guittard, El Rey, Valrhona, or the exquisite Scharffen Berger chocolate made in Berkeley, California. Since these chocolates are not always divided into 1-ounce squares, you may need a kitchen scale.

CHOOSING TYPES OF CHOCOLATE

Unless you are very experienced, you will have the best results if you stick to the type of chocolate called for in the recipe. You really have to know what you are doing to substitute bittersweet for unsweetened, and so on. Milk chocolate and white chocolate rarely substitute well for semisweet or bittersweet chocolate, unless simply used as a coating.

SWEET CHOCOLATE AND SWEET DARK CHOCOLATE

I do not use these types of chocolate for recipes.

SEMISWEET AND BITTERSWEET CHOCOLATE

Regardless of their names, standard domestic bittersweet and semisweet chocolates are interchangeable. Both usually contain 50 to 60 percent ground cocoa beans (though the legal minimum is only 35 percent) and 40 to 50 percent sugar. Generally, bittersweet is less sweet than semisweet, but the chocolate industry does not make an official distinction between them, so one brand of semisweet may or may not be sweeter than a bittersweet made by a different company. Meanwhile, the percentage of cocoa beans in the chocolate, which *does* predict sweetness, does *not* usually appear on standard domestic chocolate labels

By contrast, the best European and the newest American boutique semisweet and bittersweet chocolates often have higher cocoa bean content (and less sugar). And, the cocoa bean percentage *is* conveniently marked on the front of the wrapper. (Percentage of cocoa beans is also referred to as percentage of cacao, cocoa, cocoa solids, chocolate liquor, or cocoa masse.)

The higher the percentage of cocoa beans, the lower the sugar and the stronger and more intense the chocolate. Chocolate nibblers need only choose their octane. Indeed, high-percentage chocolates are nirvana for flavor-seeking chocolate lovers. However, cooks, confectioners and bakers should know that recipes usually need adjustment when high-percentage chocolates are used. A few recipes are instantly improved with extra chocolate intensity. But more often, chocolate with high cocoa bean content produces dry, overcooked cakes, curdled sauces, grainy ganache, and bitter, gummy mousse. The simple solution is to reduce the quantity of chocolate used and add sugar and/or liquid.

For guidance making these adjustments, consult the Chocolate Note beneath the ingredient list in most recipes that call for semisweet of bittersweet chocolate. For more about the Chocolate Notes, see page xix.

It is often possible to substitute a chopped-up bar of good chocolate for chocolate chips, but I never substitute chocolate chips for bar chocolate. When a recipe calls for bittersweet or semisweet chocolate to be melted and blended into a cake batter, chocolate mousse, or ganache, I choose bar chocolate.

MILK CHOCOLATE

Milk chocolate is used infrequently in this book; however, it is worth using a brand that you enjoy nibbling, whether imported or domestic. If you shop in specialty shops or by mail order, I highly recommend Scharffen Berger milk chocolate for its clean, fresh milk flavor and chocolate intensity. I also like Callebaut or El Rey, the former for its rich balance of caramelized creamy chocolate flavor, the latter for its complexity and earthiness.

WHITE CHOCOLATE

So-called white chocolates are not all created equal. The best white chocolate contains no other fat than cocoa butter, the natural fat in pure cocoa beans, rather than other vegetable fats such as partially hydrogenated palm kernel, palm, soy, or cottonseed oils. Because of the cocoa butter, fine white chocolate is ivory or creamy pale yellow in color, rather than pure white. Callebaut, Lindt, and especially El Rey, are my favorite brands of white chocolate.

CHOCOLATE CHIPS OR MORSELS

Chocolate chips are especially formulated for retaining their individual shape and creamy texture without burning, especially when they come in contact with a hot cookie sheet or cake pan. I use chips mostly in cookies, occasionally in cakes or loaves. I often substitute chopped-up bar chocolate for chocolate chips when I want a subtler, more sophisticated, or less sweet burst of chocolate flavor. I give options in recipes where applicable. The chocolate chip brand names that I like are Nestlé Toll House and E. Guittard. Most white chocolate chips contain very little, if any, cocoa butter, so the flavor is predominantly a sweet creamy or milky vanilla flavor at best. I prefer Guittard to other brands, but mostly I try to get away with a bar of white chocolate, hand chopped.

STORING CHOCOLATE

Semisweet, bittersweet, and unsweetened chocolate will keep for at least a year if kept cool, wrapped airtight, and protected from moisture and odors. However, I try not to keep chocolate that long. In practice, it is difficult to protect it from the air and environment if you are wrapping and rewrapping frequently. Never store packages of chocolate in the cupboard with spices or other aromatic foods (trust me on this—you don't want to try it yourself).

Milk chocolate and white chocolate get stale and develop off flavors in a much shorter period of time. Buy only what you will use within about 2 months or divide a larger quantity into portions and freeze them, wrapped airtight and enclosed in an airtight freezer bag. To avoid condensation on the chocolate, thaw it completely before unwrapping or removing it from the freezer bag.

COCOA

Cocoa powder used for baking is unsweetened and either natural—usually simply labeled unsweetened cocoa powder—or Dutch process (alkalized). Both types of cocoa are bitter when tasted alone. Natural cocoa has a fruitier, more complex chocolate flavor, which is more acidic and tart, while alkalized cocoa has a mellower, almost nutty toasted chocolate flavor. It is best to use the type of cocoa called for in the recipe, unless you are given a choice. Ghirardelli, Hershey's (brown label), and Nestlé are natural cocoas that are readily available in the supermarket. Droste is the best of the Dutch-process cocoas widely available in supermarkets. Superb-quality cocoas such as Merckens (natural or Dutch process), Scharffen Berger (natural), Valrhona (Dutch process), Pernigotti (Dutch process), Bensdorp (Dutch process), and myriad imported brands are available at specialty stores and by mail order.

equipment

BOWLS

I keep a collection of stainless-steel and glass mixing bowls on hand. Bowls that are nearly as deep as they are wide keep dry ingredients from flying out and are the best shapes for beating egg whites. Large glass measuring cups in 1- and 2-quart sizes make wonderful mixing bowls.

CAKE DECORATING TURNTABLE

A heavy, well-balanced lazy Susan is a terrific tool for frosting and decorating cakes, but a lightweight plastic one will do in a pinch. Ateco makes an excellent (but expensive) decorating turntable, which is available at restaurant supply and kitchenware stores or by mail (see page 124). A 12-inch metal banding wheel from a ceramics supply shop is as good as an Ateco at about half the cost.

CAKE PANS

I prefer medium- to heavy-weight aluminum or professional-quality steel (not stainless-steel) cake pans. For even baking and moist tender cakes, avoid pans with dark surfaces. For cake layers, cake squares, and brownies, straight- rather than slope-sided pans are best. Useful sizes are 8- and 9-inch round and square pans and 13x9-inch pans, all 2 inches deep. For springform pans, I prefer those with true 8- and 9-inch diameters and a depth of fully 3 inches rather than European pans with metric sizes. Magic Line brand pans with removable push-up bottoms are even better than traditional springforms. If substituting these for springforms (as I do), select pans 3 inches deep rather than 2 inches. If you must

bake in glass pans (I never do), remember to set the oven 25 degrees lower and check for doneness a little early, just in case.

COOKIE SHEETS AND JELLY-ROLL PANS

Medium- to heavy-weight aluminum baking sheets and jelly-roll pans will not warp or bend, and they cook evenly without hot spots. Professional aluminum half-sheet pans, which measure 16x12x1 inches, will fit most home ovens. Use them as jelly-roll pans or cookie sheets in place of the lighter-weight standard home size (17x11 inches). Buy them in restaurant supply stores—most are happy to sell to the public—or warehouse grocery discount stores or send for them from a mail-order house (see page 124). I do not like pans with dark surfaces or air-cushioned pans, even if they have specially coated nonstick surfaces.

COOLING RACKS

Racks for cooling cakes and cookies speed up the cooling process and keep some baked goods from having soggy bottoms. No need for fancy or expensive racks, just something to elevate the pan from the counter.

FOOD PROCESSOR

The processor is invaluable for pulverizing nuts or chocolate, transforming ordinary granulated sugar into extra-fine granulated for meringue making, making fruit purées, and mixing tart dough.

MEASURING CUPS

For measuring liquids, I keep 1-cup, 2-cup, 4-cup, and 8-cup measures. The largest size doubles as a mixing bowl. For measuring flour and dry ingredients, I keep at least 1 set of metal or plastic measuring cups including $1/8$, $1/4$, $1/3$, $1/2$, and 1 cup.

MICROWAVE OVEN

A microwave oven is a great tool for melting chocolate, making and reheating caramel, and raising refrigerated ingredients such as eggs, butter, and milk to room temperature (70°F.).

MIXERS

Most of the recipes in this book were tested with a hand-held portable electric mixer made by KitchenAid. A few recipes call for a stand mixer. I use a KitchenAid 5-quart mixer. I keep an extra set of beaters for both mixers so that I do not have to wash between batters and egg whites, and so on.

PARCHMENT PAPER

Baker's parchment paper is much better than grease on the bottom of a cake pan and can be used to line cookie sheets as well. Everything baked, from meringues to macaroons, releases from parchment paper.

PASTRY BAGS

Pastry bags made of nylon or polypropylene are better than cloth or canvas bags because they wash easily, remain supple, and do not become sour or malodorous. Whipped cream does not weep through these bags either. Disposable plastic pastry bags eliminate the need to wash altogether. A large 16- to 18-inch bag is handy for piping a batch of meringue. A 10- to 12-inch bag is handy for smaller quantities. Pastry bags should not be filled much more than half full; thus a bag that is a little too big is better than one that is too small.

PASTRY BRUSHES

Natural boar-bristle brushes are the best. Keep separate brushes for pastry unless you want your desserts to taste of barbecue sauce.

PASTRY TIPS

Ateco is the most pervasive brand. A useful assortment of tips would include plain round tips varying in diameter from $3/8$-inch to $11/16$-inch (Ateco #804 to #809) as well as Ateco star tips from the #820 series and the #840 series.

ROLLING PINS

With or without handles, heavy or lightweight, the pin you choose should be comfortable for you. I find that straight rather than tapered pins work best for beginners. Absent a rolling pin, improvise with a length of thick dowel or pipe or a tall bottle.

SCALE

A scale is the most accurate and simplest way to measure flour, dry ingredients, and nuts, since it enables you to weigh before sifting or grinding. Many chocolates do not come in premeasured squares, so a scale is a must in my kitchen.

SCISSORS

Keep a pair in the kitchen for cutting parchment paper and other uses.

SERRATED BREAD KNIFE

Any serrated knife is the best tool for cutting a sponge cake or genoise into thin horizontal layers, but a 12-inch blade is the best of all.

SKEWERS AND TOOTHPICKS

For testing cakes, wooden (barbecue) skewers are cleaner than broom straws and longer than toothpicks. I prefer wood skewers or toothpicks to metal cake testers. Moist batter and crumbs stick to a wood skewer better than metal, so that you can see specifically how gooey the interior of a cake is.

SPATULAS: METAL FOR ICING

For frosting cakes I like a stainless-steel spatula with a straight 8-inch-long blade rounded at the end. For spreading cake batter in a jelly-roll pan I use an offset or angled spatula (the blade has a bend in it right after the handle) with a blade at least 8 inches long.

SPATULAS: RUBBER AND HEATPROOF SILICONE

Three sizes cover every contingency. Large-size professional spatulas are the very best for folding meringue into delicate batters and scraping large bowls. A mini spatula is very handy for teasing tiny quantities from small containers and cups. Medium handles everything in between. Unless made of silicone, rubber spatulas melt and discolor if used on the stove. Silicone spatulas, on the other hand, are a miracle for stovetop cooking of everything from custards to candy. I no longer use wooden spoons on top of the stove.

STRAINERS

I use a medium-fine mesh strainer for sifting flour and dry ingredients. It can be operated with one hand and it shakes out and cleans easily. Fine-mesh strainers are best for dusting desserts with powdered sugar or cocoa. With the exception of one or two good fine-mesh stainless-steel strainers, I buy inexpensive strainers with plastic rims so that I can keep many different sizes on hand.

TART PAN WITH REMOVABLE BOTTOM

I use a 9½-inch pan with a shiny reflective surface and fluted edges, rather than one made of darkened steel.

THERMOMETERS: CANDY

A thermometer with a range that exceeds 300°F. is necessary for caramel and similar candies. Mercury candy thermometers (available in grocery and hardware stores) are inexpensive, but digital thermometers are more convenient and fun if you like gadgets. My favorite is a combination timer/thermometer made by Polder with a range of 32° to 392°F. (0° to 200°C.). It has a probe attached to a wire that can be inserted into a roast beef or loaf of bread in the oven (or a pot of candy on top of the stove). The temperature registers on a digital display that sits on the counter and can be set to beep when the desired temperature is reached.

THERMOMETERS: INSTANT-READ MEAT

Inexpensive thermometers are available in cookware and hardware stores, although you pay a little extra for digital. With a range between 0° and 220°F., these thermometers are perfect for cooking custards, working with chocolate, or determining when eggs, butter, and milk are at room temperature (70°F.) for cake baking.

THERMOMETERS: OVEN

Even the best recipes suffer from baking at the wrong temperatures. Use the thermometer to check your oven every now and again to see that it is accurate and either have it adjusted or compensate for the error yourself until you can have someone adjust it properly.

TIMER

Whether it's a tick-tick-ding-ding or a digital buzzer, you've got to have one.

WIRE WHISKS

Whisks are better than kitchen forks for mixing dry ingredients together and fluffing up the flour before you add it to the batter and for generally whisking things together.

ZESTER

The new Microplane citrus zester is a dream tool to lift off only the thinnest layer of finely shredded zest.

resources

RETAIL AND MAIL-ORDER SOURCES

King Arthur Flour
The Baker's Catalogue
P.O. Box 876
Norwich, VT 05055-0876
1.800.827.6836

Retail store and mail-order catalog.
*Everything for the baker and dessert
maker. Cocoas, various chocolates,
crystallized ginger, gold leaf and gold
powder (petal dust), and much more.*

Parrish's Cake Decorating Supply, Inc.
225 West 146th Street
Gardena, CA 90248
1.800.736.8443

Retail store and mail-order catalog.
*Everything for the baker including
Magic Line pans with solid or removable
bottoms in every conceivable size, both
2 inches and 3 inches deep.*

Scharffen Berger Chocolate Maker, Inc.
(factory and retail store)
914 Heinz Avenue
Berkeley, CA 94710
800.930.4528
www.Scharffen-Berger.com

Sugar and Spice
2965 Junipero Serra Boulevard
Daly City, CA 94014
1.650.994.4911

*Supplies for cake decorators and
candy makers, including silica gel.*

Sur La Table
Pike Place Market
Seattle, WA 98134-1608
206.448.2244

Mail-order catalog and retail stores
across the country.
*Quality tools and equipment for home
bakers. Gold leaf and gold powder
for decorating. Scharffen Berger and
Valrhona chocolate.*

Sweet Celebrations
(Formerly Maid of Scandinavia)
7009 Washington Avenue. S
Edina, MN 55439
1.800.328.6722

Mail-order catalog.
*Ingredients and equipment for the
home baker.*

Williams-Sonoma
P.O. Box 7456
San Francisco, CA 94120
1.800.541.2233

Retail stores across the country and
mail-order catalog.
*Baking tools and equipment. Pernigotti
cocoa; Scharffen Berger, Valrhona, and
Callebaut chocolates; crystallized ginger.*

Don't forget:

Local natural-foods and health-food
stores for nuts, dried fruits, organic flour,
unsweetened coconut, and spices.

Art supply stores or Indian grocery stores
for 22- and 23-carat gold leaf (called
Vark in Indian groceries) for decorating.

Ceramics supply stores for banding
wheels to use as decorating turntables.

Restaurant supply stores for half-sheet
pans and cake pans, Ateco decorating
turntables, and more.

index

Almond extract, 114

Almonds
    on Boardwalk Bananas, 89
    brittle, 110
    caramel-glazed, 110
    in Chocolate-Laced Holiday Stollen, 48–49
    gold-and-silver-coated, 109
    in Independence Day Sundaes, 86
    in Mocha Marjolaine, 7–8
    in nut-and-caramel lace cookie cups, 86
    in Passover Chocolate Nut Sponge Torte, 66
    in Passover Gâteau au Chocolat, 67
    on Ripe Figs with Mint Ganache, 15
    on White Chocolate–Banana Nectarine Trifle, 98

Apples, Chocolate-Dipped Caramel, 24

Apricot Orange Wedding Cakes, 81

Artificial flavorings, 114

Ateco products, 120, 121

Autumn recipes, 1–25

Babka, Chocolate Cranberry, 42

Baking basics, the importance of, xiv–xix

Baking powder and soda, 114

Bananas
    Boardwalk (chocolate-dipped frozen), 89
    Chocolate Blintzes, 28

Chocolate Waffles, 83
    White Chocolate–Nectarine Trifle, 98

Bar chocolate, chocolate chips vs., 108, 117, 118

Basic Caramel, 111

Basket, Chocolate, 70

Bensdorp cocoa, 118

Bittersweet chocolate, 117
    storage of, 118

Bittersweet Chocolate Truffles, 38
    in Chocolate Easter Baskets, 70

Black-and-White Apricot Pecan Cake, 44–45

Blackberries
    Hazelnut Chocolate Meringue with, 103
    on Independence Day Sundaes, 86
    in Mini Caramel Cheesecakes, 90
    in White Chocolate–Banana Nectarine Trifle, 98

Blini, Chocolate with Berry Caviar, 46

Blintzes, Chocolate Banana, 28

Blueberries, on Independence Day Sundaes, 86

Boardwalk Bananas, 89

Bowls, mixing, 120, 121

Bread pudding, Chocolate Cranberry, 13

Breakfast Valentines, 51

Brioche, Chocolate Cranberry, 42

Brownies
    ice bath/freezer method, 65
    Passover, 65

Brown sugar, recommendations and tips, 116

Bûche de Noël, Chocolate Hazelnut, 36–37

Burnt chocolate, dealing with, xvii

Butter
    bringing to room temperature, xviii, 121
    melting chocolate with, xvii
    unsalted, 114

C&H cane sugar, 115–16

Cake decorating, 108–11
    metal spatula for icing, 122
    turntable for, 120

Cake pans, 120
    parchment paper lining, 121

Cakes
    Apricot Orange Wedding Cakes, 81
    Black-and-White Apricot Pecan Cake, 44–45
    Chocolate Peanut Butter Layer Cake, 2
    Chocolate Pound Cake, 97
    Chocolate Sour Cream Cake, 4–5
    Fastest Fudge Cake, 104
    Flourless Chocolate Cake, 57–58
    Gingerbread with Milk Chocolate Chunks, 16
    Mini Blackberry Caramel Cheesecake, 90
    Mocha Marble Cheesecake, 69

Cakes (continued)

Mocha Marjolaine, 7–8

Passover Brownies, 65

Passover Chocolate Nut Sponge Torte, 66

Passover Gâteau au Chocolat, 67

White Chocolate–Banana Nectarine
Trifle, 98

White Chocolate–Lemon Cheesecake, 79

Callebaut chocolate, 116

milk chocolate, 117

white chocolate, 79, 82, 94, 99, 118

Candy thermometer, 122–23

Cane sugar, 115–16

Caramel

basic preparation, 111

Chocolate Cream Puffs with Spun
Sugar, 32–34

Chocolate-Dipped Apples, 24

decorations, 110

as glaze, 110

Mini Blackberry Cheesecakes, 90

-nut lace cookie cups, 86

shards and shapes, 110

on Winter Solstice Cookies, 30

Caramel-Glazed Nuts, 110

on Honey Walnut Tart, 10–12

Cheesecake

Mini Blackberry Caramel, 90

Mocha Marble, 69

White Chocolate Lemon, 79

Chocolate

bar vs. chips., 108, 117, 118

brands of, 116–18

dessert decorations, 108–9

melting technique, xvi–vii, 108–9

storage of, 117

tempering procedure, 112–13

types of, 116–17

Chocolate Banana Blintzes, 28

Chocolate Banana Waffles for Dad, 83

Chocolate Blini with Berry Caviar, 46

Chocolate chips, 118

bar chocolate vs., 108, 117, 118

in Chocolate Cranberry Babka, 42

in Chocolate-Laced Holiday Stollen, 48

in Hazelnut Chocolate Meringue with
Blackberries, 103

recommended brands, 118

Chocolate Coconut Macaroons, 31

Chocolate Cranberry Babka, 42

Chocolate Cranberry Bread Pudding, 13

Chocolate Cream Puffs with Spun Sugar,
32–33

Chocolate curls, 108

Chocolate-Dipped Caramel Apples, 24

Chocolate-Dipped Strawberries, 78

Chocolate Easter Baskets, 70

Chocolate Hamantaschen, 62–64

Chocolate Hazelnut Roulade, 35–36

Chocolate-Laced Holiday Stollen, 48–49

Chocolate Latkes, 31

Chocolate Leaves, 109

on Mocha Marjolaine, 7–8

Chocolate Mardi Gras Fondue, 59

Chocolate Notes, about, xix

Chocolate Peanut Butter Layer Cake, 2

Chocolate Pecan Pie, 18–19

Chocolate Piping, 108–9

Chocolate Pound Cake, 97

Chocolate Rum Custard, 32–33

Chocolate Sauce, 88

on Independence Day Sundaes, 86

Chocolate Sour Cream Layer Cake, 4–5

Chocolate Peanut Butter Layer Cake, 2

Christmas, desserts for

Bittersweet Chocolate Truffles, 38

Chocolate Cream Puffs with Spun
Sugar, 32–33

Chocolate-Laced Stollen, 48–49

Cocoa butter, 117, 118

Cocoa powder, 117

in Bittersweet Chocolate Truffles, 38

in Black-and-White Apricot Pecan
Cake, 44–45

in Breakfast Valentines, 51

in Chocolate Banana Waffles, 83

in Chocolate Blini with Berry Caviar,
46

in Chocolate Pound Cake, 97

in Chocolate Sour Cream Layer Cake, 4–5

in Fastest Fudge Cake, 104

in Fast Fudge Frosting, 105

in Hot Waffle Ice Cream Sandwiches, 100

in Maya's Day of the Dead Cookies, 22

Coconut, in Chocolate Latkes, 31

Coffee instant powder, 114

Coffee Meringue Mushrooms, 71

in Chocolate Easter Baskets, 70

Confectioners' sugar, 116

Cookies

Chocolate Hamantaschen, 62–64

Chocolate Latkes, 31

as Independence Day Sundae cups, 86

Maya's Day of the Dead, 22–23

nut-and-caramel lace cups, 86

Passover Brownies, 65

Winter Solstice, 30

Cookie sheets, 120

parchment paper lining, 121

Cooling baked items, xix

brownie ice bath/freezer method, 65

Cooling racks, 120

Cranberries

in Chocolate Bread Pudding, 13

in Chocolate Cranberry Babka, 42

Cream, 114

Cream puffs

Chocolate with Spun Sugar, 32–33

Ice Cream Easter Eggs, 74–75

Crepes

Chocolate Banana Blintzes, 28

Chocolate Blini with Berry Caviar, 46

Croquembouche, Chocolate Cream Puffs with Spun Sugar, 32

Cupcakes, Apricot Orange Wedding Cakes, 81

Curls, chocolate, 108

Custard, Chocolate Rum, 32–33

Custard Sauce, White Chocolate, 99

Dark brown sugar, 116

Dark chocolate. *See* Chocolate

Decorating techniques, 108–11

equipment, 120, 121, 122

Desiccants, 110

Details, importance of, xiv–xix

Digital thermometer, 123

Dipped fruits

Boardwalk Bananas, 89

Chocolate-Dipped Caramel Apples, 24

Chocolate-Dipped Strawberries, 78

in Chocolate Mardi Gras Fondue, 59

Disposable plastic pastry bags, 121

Dolce de leche ice cream, in Hot Waffle Sandwiches, 100

Double boiler, for melting chocolate, xvii

Dragées, 109

Dried Apricots, in Black-and-White Pecan Cake, 44–45

Dried Cranberries

in Chocolate Babka, 42

in Chocolate Bread Pudding, 13

Dried fruits, 114

in Chocolate-Laced Holiday Stollen, 48–49

as Chocolate Mardi Gras Fondue dippers, 59

Droste cocoa, 118

Dry ingredients

blending into batter, xviii

measuring, xvi, 121

Dutch-process cocoa, 118. *See also* Cocoa powder

Easter

Chocolate Easter Baskets, 70

Giant Krispy Egg, 76

Ice Cream Easter Eggs, 74–75

Edible flowers, 81

Eggs, 114

bringing to room temperature, xviii, 114, 121

E. Guittard chocolate, 116

chocolate chips, 118

Electric mixer, xviii, 121

El Rey chocolate, 116, 117, 118

   milk chocolate, 117

   white chocolate, 79, 82, 94, 99, 118

Equipment, xvi, 120–23

Espresso instant powder, 114

Extracts

   liquor, 115

   pure vs. artificial flavorings, 114

Extra-fine granulated sugar, 116, 120

Fastest Fudge Cake, 104

Fast Fudge Frosting, 105

   on Fastest Fudge Cake, 104

Fast Fudge Glaze, on Ice Cream Easter

   Eggs, 74–75

Father's Day, Chocolate Banana Waffles,

   83

Figs (ripe), Mint Ganache, 16

Fine granualaged sugar, 116

Flour, 115

   blending in, xviii

   measuring, xv–xvi

   sifting, xv, xvi

Flourless Chocolate Cake, 57–58

Fondue, Mardi Gras, 59

Food processor, xvii, 120

   pulverizing nuts in, 115, 120

Fourth of July, Independence Day

   Sundaes, 86

Freezing

   brownie quick-cooling method, 65

   chocolate-dipped bananas, 89

   milk and white chocolate, 118

Fritters, Honey-Drizzled Chocolate

   Cheese, 9

Frosting

   Chocolate Sour Cream, 4

   Fastest Fudge, 105

   spatulas for, 122

Fruits. *See* Dipped fruits; Dried fruits;

   See also specific types

Fudge Cake, 104

Fudge Frosting, 105

Fudge Glaze, 74

Ganache

   Mocha Marjolaine, 7–8

   Ripe Figs with Mint, 15

Gâteau au Chocolat, Passover, 67

Genoise, White Chocolate Banana

   Nectarine Trifle, 98

Ghiradelli chocolate, 116

   milk chocolate, 117

Ghiradelli cocoa powder, 118

Giant Krispy Egg, 76

Gilding technique, 109

Gingerbread with Milk Chocolate Chunks, 16

Glass bowls, 120

Glazes

   Caramel, 110

   Fast Fudge, 74

   Honey and Bittersweet Chocolate, 10

   White Chocolate, 82

Golden (light) brown sugar, 115–16

Gold leaf and powder, 109

   on Apricot Orange Wedding Cakes, 81

Granulated sugar, 115–16, 120

Hamantaschen, Chocolate, 62–64

Hand-held electric mixer, 121

Hanukkah, Honey-Drizzled Chocolate

   Fritters, 9

Hazan, Marcella, 9

Hazelnut Chocolate Meringue with

   Blackberries, 103

Hazelnuts

   on Boardwalk Bananas, 89

   Brittle, 110

   Caramel-Glazed, 110

   in Chocolate Roulade, 35–36

   in Mocha Marjolaine, 7–8

Hershey's (brown label) cocoa, 118

Honey-Drizzled Chocolate Cheese

   Fritters, 9

Honey Walnut Tart, 10–12

Hot Chocolate, 41

Hot Chocolate Soufflés, 52–53

Hot Waffle Ice Cream Sandwiches, 100

Ice Cream
   Hot Waffle Sandwiches, 100
   Independence Day Sundaes, 86
Ice Cream Easter Eggs, 74–75
Icing. See Frosting
Independence Day Sundaes, 86
Individual cakes
   Apricot Orange Weeding Cakes, 81
   Honey Walnut Tart, 10–12
   Mini Blackberry Caramel Cheesecakes, 90
   Passover Brownies, 65
   See also Cookies
Ingredients, 114–18
Instant coffee. See Coffee instant powder;
   Espresso instant powder
Instant-read meat thermometer, 123
Irish Coffee Chocolate Mousse, 54

Jelly-roll pans, 120
Jewish dietary laws, 114

KitchenAid electric mixers, 121
Klein, Maya, 22

Latkes, Chocolate, 31
Lazy Susan, for cake frosting/decoration,
   120
Leaf, gold and silver, 109
Leaves, chocolate, 109
Lemon, White Chocolate–Cheesecake, 79

Light (golden) brown sugar, 115–16
Lindt chocolate, 118
   white chocolate, 79, 82, 94, 99, 118
Liqueurs, 115
Liquid measures, xvi, 121

Macaroons, Chocolate Coconut, 31
Magic Line cake pans, 120
Marbled cakes
   Black-and-White Apricot Pecan Cake,
   44–45
   Mocha Cheesecake, 69
Margarine, 114
Maya's Day of the Dead Cookies, 22–23
Measurement, xv–xvi
   brown sugar, 116
Measuring cups, xvi, 121
   as mixing bowls, 120, 121
Melting chocolate, xvi–vii, 108–9
   bar preferred for, 108, 117
   burned and seized, xvii
   microwave oven for, xvii, 121
Merckens cocoa, 118
Meringue
   Coffee Mushrooms, 71
   Hazelnut Chocolate with Blackberries, 103
   in Mocha Marjolaine, 7–8
   Strawberry Mocha, 93
Metal banding wheel, 120
Metal spatulas, 122

Microplane citrus zester, 123
Microwave oven, xviii, 121
   for melting chocolate, xvii, 121
Michel Cluizel chocolate, 116
Milk, bringing to room temperature, xviii,
   121
Milk chocolate, 117
   for Chocolate-Dipped Strawberries, 78
   chopping and melting, xvii
   chunks in gingerbread, 16
   Giant Krispy Egg, 76
   in Mocha Marble Cheesecake, 69
   storage of, 118
Mini Blackberry Caramel Cheesecakes, 90
Mint
   in New Strawberries and Cream, 94
   Ripe Figs Ganache with, 16
Mise en place (setting up), xiv–xv
Mixers, electric, xviii, 121
Mixing bowls, 120, 121
Mixing method, xvii–viii
Mocha, Strawberry Meringue, 93
Mocha Marble Cheesecake, 69
Mocha Marjolaine, 7–8
Mousse, Irish Coffee Chocolate, 54
Mushrooms, Coffee Meringue, 71

Natural cocoa, 118
Nectarines, White Chocolate–Banana
   Trifle, 98

Nestlé cocoa, 118

Nestlé Toll House chocolate chips, 118

New Strawberries and Cream, The, 94

New Year's Day, desserts for

Chocolate Blini with Berry Caviar, 46

Honey Walnut Tart, 10–12

New Year's Eve, desserts for

Chocolate Blini with Berry Caviar, 46

Chocolate Cream Puffs with

Spun Sugar, 32–33

Nuts, 115

brittle, 110

caramel-glazed, 110

pulverizing, 115, 120

toasting method, 115

See also specific types

Order of ingredients, importance in mixing,

xviii

Oven

preheating, xix

rack placement, xix

thermometer, 123

Pans, 120, 121

Parchment paper, 121

Pareve unsalted margarine, 114

Passover, desserts for

Passover Brownies, 65

Passover Chocolate Coconut

Macaroons, 31

Passover Chocolate Nut Sponge Torte, 66

Passover Gâteau au Chocolat, 67

Pastry bags, 121

Pastry brushes, 121

Pastry tips, 121

Peanut Brittle, 110

in Chocolate Peanut Butter Layer Cake, 2

Peanut Butter, Chocolate Layer Cake, 2–3

Peanuts

on Boardwalk Bananas, 89

in Chocolate Peanut Butter Layer Cake, 2

Pecans

in Black-and-White Apricot Pecan

Cake, 44–45

brittle, 110

caramel-glazed, 110

in Chocolate Pecan Pie, 18–19

in Passover Brownies, 65

Peppermint

in New Strawberries and Cream, 94

in Ripe Figs Ganache, 15

Pernigotti cocoa, 118

Pie, Chocolate Pecan, 18–19

Piping, chocolate, 109

Plastic pastry bags, 121

Polder thermometer, 123

Pound Cake, Chocolate, 97

Powder, gold and silver, 109

Powdered sugar, 116

Prebaked pie crust, heating filling for, 18

Preheating oven, xix

Presifting, xv

Pretzel sticks, chocolate-coated, 70

Profiteroles, Ice Cream Easter Eggs,

74–75

Pudding, Chocolate Cranberry Bread, 13

Pulverizing nuts, 115

Pure extracts, 114

Purim, Chocolate Hamantaschen for,

62–64

Racks, cooling, 120

Raspberries

in Chocolate Blini with Berry Caviar, 46

Flourless Chocolate Cake with, 56–58

Passover Gâteau au Chocolat with, 67

on Ripe Figs with Mint Ganache, 15

Ripe Figs with Mint Ganache, 15

Rolling pins, 121

Room temperature

bringing ingredients to, xviii, 114, 121

instant-read thermometer, 123

Rosh Hashanah, desserts for

Gingerbread with Milk Chocolate

Chunks, 16

Honey-Drizzled Chocolate Fritters, 9

Honey Walnut Tart, 10–12

Roulade, Chocolate Hazelnut, 35–36

Rubber spatulas, 122

Rum

in Chocolate Custard Cream Puffs,
32–33

in Chocolate Pecan Pie, 18–19

in White Chocolate–Banana Nectarine
Trifle, 98

Sauces

Chocolate, 88

Fast Fudge, 105

Raspberry, 57

White Chocolate Custard, 99

Scale, kitchen, 121–22

Scharffen Berger chocolate, 116, 117

Scharffen Berger cocoa, 118

Schmidt, Stephen, 18

Scissors, 122

Seized chocolate, xvii

Semisweet chocolate, 117

storage of, 118

Sequencing, importance in baking of,
xiv–xv, xviii

Serrated bread knife, 122

Setting up, xiv–xv

Shards and shapes, caramel, 110

Shavings, chocolate, 108

Shot, decorating with, 109

Sifting, xv, xvi

Silicone spatulas, 122

Silver Leaf and Powder, 109

Skewers, 122

Soufflés, Hot Chocolate, 52–53

Sour cream, in Chocolate Layer Cake, 4–5

Spatulas, xvii, 122

Spices, 115

Spirits, 115. *See also specific types*

Sponge Torte, Passover Chocolate Nut, 66

Springform cake pans, 120

Spring recipes, 61–83

Spun Sugar, 111

on Chocolate Cream Puffs, 32–33

Stainless steel bowls, 120

Stencils, 109–10

Stollen, Chocolate-Laced, 48–49

Storing chocolate, 118

Strainers, 122

Strawberries

Chocolate-Dipped, 78

on Independence Day Sundaes, 86

in White Chocolate Mint Cream, 94

Strawberry Mocha Meringue, 93

Substitutions, chocolate, 117

Sugar, 115–16

pulverizing, 116, 120

spun preparation, 111

Sundaes, Independence Day, 86

Superfine granulated sugar, 116

Sweet and sweet dark chocolate, 117

Tarts

Honey Walnut, 10–12

removable-bottom pan for, 122

Temperature

of ingredients, xviii

oven, xix

thermometer types, 122–23

Tempering chocolate, 112–13

Tenderness in baking, achieving, xiv–xv

Texture, temperature of ingredients and,
xviii

Thanksgiving, Chocolate Cranberry Bread
Pudding, 13

Thermometers, 122–23

Timers, 123

Toasting nuts, 115

Tobler white chocolate, 99

Tools. *See* Equipment

Toothpicks, 122

Torte, Passover Chocolate Nut Sponge, 66

Toughness in baked products, reasons
for, xiv–xv, xviii, 116

Trifle, White Chocolate–Banana Nectarine,
98

Truffles, Bittersweet Chocolate, 38

Turntable, for cake frosting/decorating,
120

Ultimate Flourless Chocolate Cake, The, 57–58
Unsalted butter, 114
Unsweetened chocolate
    in Chocolate Hamantaschen, 62
    in Passover Brownies, 65
    storage of, 118

Valentines, Breakfast, 50
Valrhona chocolate, 116
    cocoa, 118
    milk chocolate, 117
    white chocolate, 79, 82, 94, 99
Very Rich Hot Chocolate, 41

Waffles
    Chocolate Banana, 83
    Hot Ice Cream Sandwiches, 100
Walnuts
    brittle, 110
    caramel-glazed, 110

Tart, Honey, 10–12
    in Passover Brownies, 65
Water-bath method, melting chocolate, xvii
Wedding cakes, Apricot Orange Cup Cakes, 81
Whiskey
    in Black-and-White Apricot Pecan Cake, 44–45
    in Chocolate Pecan Pie, 18–19
    Irish Coffee Chocolate Mousse, 54
    See also Rum
Whisks, wire, 123
White chocolate, 117–18
    for Chocolate-Dipped Strawberries, 78
    chopping and melting, xvii
    drawbacks of chips, 118
    Giant Krispy Egg, 76
    good-quality brands, 79, 82, 94, 99
    melting technique, 109
    in Mini Blackberry Caramel Cheesecakes, 90

    in New Strawberries and Cream, 94
    storage of, 118
    in Strawberry Mocha Meringue, 93
White Chocolate–Banana Nectarine Trifle, 98
White Chocolate Cream, 93
White Chocolate Custard Sauce, 99
    in White Chocolate–Banana Nectarine Trifle, 98
White Chocolate Glaze, 82
    on Apricot Orange Wedding Cakes, 81
    on Ice Cream Easter Eggs, 74–75
White Chocolate–Lemon Cheesecake, 79
Winter Solstice Cookies, 30
Wire whisks, 123
Wrapping, xix

Zester, 123